# My Daddy Died

## Supporting young children in grief

**Heather Teakle**

GW00633909

CollinsDove
A Division of HarperCollins*Publishers*

Published by Collins Dove
A Division of HarperCollins*Publishers* (Australia) Pty Ltd
22–24 Joseph Street
North Blackburn Victoria 3130

First published 1992
Designed by John Canty
Cover design by Tom Kurema
Cover photograph by Bill Thomas

Typeset in Australia by CollinsDove*Publishers*
Printed in Australia by Griffin Paperbacks

The National Library of Australia
Cataloguing-in-Publication Data:

Teakle, Heather
    My daddy died: supporting young children in grief.

ISBN 1 86371 095 7.

1. Grief in children. 2. Children and death. I. Title.

155.937

# Contents

To Evania
my little teacher

# Introduction

There is literature covering most aspects of death, grief, the dying, the bereaved. Although there is a small collection for older children, sadly I have been unable to find anything to support parents whose children are very young, who are almost, or are indeed, at a pre-verbal level of development. It is as though they are not supposed to grieve.

My motivation for writing this book, and the urgency in doing so, was a result of my own agonising, fruitless search for literature to help me work with my children in relation to the loss of their father. The awareness that other parents are out there searching in this desert for practical help, that there are little ones in need of active support in their grieving, gave urgency to the task.

Having said that my primary focus in writing is the grieving parent, I trust that the book will help the teachers and other professionals who will become involved with the families for whom I am writing. This applies in particular to the comments which are addressed specifically to professionals.

I began writing the book in the Blue Mountains near Sydney, in the home which David and I built in the place which was a symbol of our life together. It was a place of great peace and the silence and beauty of the forest nourished and supported me as I wrote.

I write this introduction in another such environment, though very different to that of the Blue Mountains. We have recently moved to our new home on the north coast of New South Wales. Here we have our own little patch of rain forest and again I take strength from the peace and beauty of our surroundings.

Since beginning writing, Geoff—whom I mention in Chapter 6 of the book—and I have married and we are looking forward to the birth of our baby in a few weeks. Evania and Ketorah are at school and pre-school and as the weeks and months fly by become more beautiful in appearance and personality. We are all reaping the fruits, I believe, of the active involvement in our grief during that most tragic time of our lives.

## Spirituality

It may help to set out a little about the spiritual dimension of my life, for much of what I will say comes out of my belief in, and experience of, that.

I am from a Christian background and in the last ten years I have become interested in the more mystical aspects of the Christian faith, and of the other great religions. I am particularly interested in Sufism, the mystical part of the Muslim faith.

In 1982 I left full-time employment to live a more contemplative life in a little village on the outskirts of Melbourne and my days were spent in relative silence and solitude. I used my time for meditation, prayer and reading, and in the second year there I spent about twenty hours a week painting Icons in the monastic tradition of the Orthodox Church. Painting, or more correctly 'writing', an Icon is a spiritual discipline, a form of meditation.

From there I went to the Blue Mountains in New South

Wales to participate in a course which was to include re-birthing, sandplay, dreams, mythology and symbolism. It was at that time that I met David.

My sense today is that I am much more in touch with the Divine within me. As a result, the 'externals' of religion, whether Christian or otherwise, are now much less important to me. I believe that all of those externals guided and supported me on my journey to discover the Divine within me and as I become more in touch with that, the external framework increasingly becomes less significant.

I continue to paint Icons, and the symbolism and ritual of the Christian Church and of other religions nourish me in new and fresh ways.

## 'Process' and 'Work'

I will often refer to 'the process', 'my process', 'the children's process', 'the grief process'. The meaning of 'process' in this context is the movement that is occurring in our inner lives, emotionally and spiritually, and as it affects our thinking, as well as its influence on our 'outer' lives. Our grief may be such that our energy level is very low and we are barely able to function in the practical matters of daily life. That is part of the grief process. It **is** a process, a forward movement. Although it may not seem so when we are in the midst of it, it does take us to our destination if we remain in it.

The analogy of a river may be helpful here. If we allow ourselves to be carried along in the middle of the stream we will be taken to our destination: the sea or perhaps a lake. Sometimes it may seem that we are going to drown before we reach our destination. The river is moving too rapidly and we are being tossed about relentlessly. We may need to cling to an overhanging branch for a time to catch our breath before letting go to continue being carried along by the stream. If we are prepared to remain in the current we will, I can assure you, 'get there'. It is not true that 'time heals'. Time of itself most certainly does not heal. If you resist the process, all that time will do is push the grief deeper into the unconscious, to grow there like a cancer until one day, maybe many years further on, it can no longer be contained. It is then much more difficult to deal with than it would have been if the grieving person had allowed herself or himself to stay with the process at the time of the bereavement.

**Only** by staying in the process will there be healing. I suspect that very few of us are free of unresolved grief, for very few of us have been allowed, or have allowed ourselves, to grieve fully rather than opt out of the process at some stage before it was complete.

The other word I use often is 'work'. It refers here again to our inner life and how we deal with what is going on there. If I am working on my anger, it means that I am examining it to see what it is about, where it comes from—the source of it is more often in the past than in the present—and how that pattern of reacting can be broken.

Anger is a natural, healthy part of the grief process, the emphasis being on the word 'process', a forward movement. If you are not moving through your anger, rather are stuck in it, then the anger is most likely related to something unresolved in your past, and you will need to examine it closely to perhaps seek some support from a therapist who can help you see more clearly what it is about and what can be done about it.

That is what I refer to as 'work'. It is what I mean when I talk about working with someone. It does not mean mixing concrete together, or gardening! It is the inner work.

Having clarified those matters, we can now continue our journey together.

# Prologue

I begin this task with a good deal of apprehension.

The sense is of awe, of something holy. I have lit a candle, incense is burning in the room and fresh flowers are arranged on my desk. It is like preparing to work on an Icon, to meditate, to pray.

Why this sense of awe? I am sure much of it is to do with the journey I will make in writing this little book, re-living our experience, a great deal of it very painful. As I write I may be taken to new levels of grief, for it is not two years since David's death and the grieving process continues.

There is no doubt that the process for each of the children will deepen during this time, as their understanding changes and grows. We will be living each day the very things about which I am writing.

As well as the apprehension about what may await us, I look forward to the healing which will come to us during the course of this writing. And I take with me on my own journey the awareness of those parents who will read this book while in similar circumstances. I am aware of their pain and anguish. My heart aches for them and as I write my tears flow for them.

*　　*　　*

My dear friends, be assured of my love as you walk this path. It is perhaps the most painful part of your journey in this life. You are trying to deal with your own grief while at the same time caring for very young, dependent children who also need support in their grief. Perhaps you will at times, as I did, resent your parental role. Perhaps you will long to be without the responsibility of the children so that you can have time and space to grieve without distraction, to 'go to pieces' without having to be together enough to look after them.

Very young children are demanding enough of your emotional, physical and spiritual resources. Grieving over the loss of your partner is on its own totally demanding of those same resources. To be dealing with both at the same time is unthinkable. Even now I wonder how I made it through that first year.

I did. You will also.

# 1. 'There's been a fatal accident...'

The words of the police officer still ring in my ears like a mantra, almost two years after I first heard them.

Evania, whose second birthday had been celebrated eleven days before, and Ketorah, five months old the previous day, were sitting beside me when those words heralded so dramatic a change in our lives.

Within a few moments I had spelled it out to the children. 'Daddy has died. He was hit by a car and so badly hurt that he died straight away. He will never be coming home again.'

What does a two-year-old understand from such a statement?

Who knows? I had to trust that providing I was honest and open and made clear statements about what had happened, Evania would make for herself some sense of the truth.

Heaven knows it is difficult enough for adults to grasp, to believe the unbelievable, to take in the reality that one's partner, parent, child, brother, sister is never again going to walk through the door.

David and I had always talked to the children about what was happening. From the time they were conceived the little ones were as much a reality, a presence in our lives, as they were after birth. We talked to them about what was happening for us, how we were feeling, what the dog was doing! When it became clear shortly before Evania's birth that I was to have a caesarian section, we talked to her about that, explaining why it was necessary and preparing her as best we could for this unnatural entrance into the world.

So telling Evania and Ketorah of their father's death and its immediate implications was a spontaneous response.

I am certain that most of us greatly underestimate how much a child senses or understands of the truth if we communicate it to them in an open and honest fashion.

There is a great deal of resistance, particularly in our parents' generation, to being honest with children, keeping them informed about what is happening. This is especially so where it involves a painful situation. Rather than protecting the children, it increases their confusion and pain. There is no doubt that most of us carry the wounds of much misguided 'protection'.

As a child I had a physical disability which resulted in many medical procedures, including surgery. My parents, believing that they were doing their best for me, said nothing of these events until that moment at the door of the hospital, or the doctor's surgery. There was no discussion about what was to happen, was happening or had happened.

The reality is that children cope remarkably well with difficult and painful situations, more so than adults in most instances, **if** there is open communication.

I have noticed this with Evania in everyday events. If I am to go out at night after the children go to sleep, I tell them beforehand that I am going out, who will be with them, and other details which may seem irrelevant to some adults. On the rare occasions when I have not done this and Evania has woken while I have been away, she has been very distressed. In contrast are those other occasions when she returns to sleep, peaceful and secure.

Similarly, when Evania was hospitalised I told her about each procedure beforehand, with one exception. During all but this unprepared-for procedure Evania was relaxed and the experience without trauma for her. During the remaining test she was extremely distressed, though the procedure itself was, objectively, less traumatic than some of the others.

Yesterday evening Ketorah gashed her head. How refreshing it was to hear the sister at the Katoomba Hospital explaining everything to the two-year-old as she treated the wound. There was no 'talking down' and Ketorah responded with interest and a complete absence of distress.

'If only they had told me what was going on!' I have heard that cry so often from adults recalling the separation of parents, the death of a loved one, their own illness or that of a member of the family. How many times have I heard them relate their childhood anguish, confusion, fear, in the absence of clear communication from adults about what was happening.

The wounds caused by that lack of information, sometimes even misinformation, remain with us into adulthood, distorting our perception of reality and our response to it. The greatest tragedy, the most profound distortion, is our inability to trust our own sense of 'knowing'. In childhood we sensed or knew that 'something was going on' and yet adult communication denied that. Where are we left then in terms of trusting our intuition? 'I sense this and they communicate that, so how can I trust my own sense of the truth when those on whom I am totally dependent are communicating this other reality?'

As each incident compounds this confusion, we lose touch more and more with our own truth. Our sense of our own worth suffers correspondingly. A vague, or maybe not so vague, distrust of others develops along with this distrust of our own knowing. What do they really mean? Is that the whole story? Can I be sure that what she is saying is the truth? What is she leaving out?

All this may or may not be occurring at a conscious level. We may rationalise it away, declaring, 'It pays to be cautious. You can't be too careful these days.' We support each other in our dis-ease. If challenged about it, we can raise an army of supporters, none of whom is any more willing than we are to look at the attitude and its origins. Insidiously it permeates our society. It grows like a cancer until, for some, it takes so much energy that they cease to live, rather merely exist.

Of course there are other factors from early experience which contribute to our disease of mistrust. I emphasise this particular aspect in order to encourage you to be completely open with your children.

Today it made me very sad to hear someone suggest, 'Later on you will be able to talk to your children about it (David and his death).'

'We talk about it all the time,' I responded.

'Oh, you are able to now, are you?'

'Now? I always have!'

I am deeply saddened to know that there are many people who feel that they are not able to share such a profound experience with their children. Tragically, the parents as well as the little ones are the losers.

# 2 Cry with me

Bereavement can be a very isolating experience in our society. As a result of our unhealthy attitudes to death people withdraw from the bereaved, more and more so as the days run into weeks and the weeks into months.

For some this withdrawal results from their own fears about death: to be with the bereaved can be a very confronting experience. Others withdraw because they think they do not know what to say or do in being with the grieving one. In our world, worth is very much associated with doing and saying. If we are not doing or saying something how can we possibly be worth anything in the situation!

So we have much to learn about the value of just **being**. What a precious thing it is for one who is grieving to have someone who is simply there for **them**, without rushing around doing things, chatting inanely or offering unsolicited advice.

I cannot emphasise more strongly the importance of being there, without feeling the need to say or do anything. If you open your mouth only for the sake of saying something, then for heaven's sake close it again, leaving what was almost certainly nonsense unsaid.

Writing about the importance of speaking clearly to your children about what is happening, I became increasingly aware of how few adults address each other plainly about these issues. The police officers who came to tell me about David's death were very caring and sensitive. They volunteered what detail they had about the accident. They did not, however, actually say 'He is dead' or 'He died' but only 'There's been a fatal accident.' It took me what seemed like an age to realise that they were telling me that David had died.

In another situation where someone had been missing for several days before being found dead, the police officer broke the news by saying only "I'm sorry'. Again the words 'dead', 'died', 'death' were avoided. It may be thought harsh to use those words. On the contrary, I believe that it is helpful. The pain is no less intense for not speaking out the fact: the bereaved needs to hear the reality.

Similarly, when the grieving person meets someone who knows about the death and fails to refer to it at all, unnecessary difficulties are created. In contrast, it does indeed lighten a little the burden of grief when the other person takes the initiative. It is so simple: 'I was sorry to hear of David's death' or 'I've been thinking of you since I heard that David had died'.

I wish I could express more adequately how alienating and painful it is when people fail to acknowledge the tragedy which has shattered your life.

People also withdraw from the bereaved because they have unresolved grief themselves. Perhaps at the time of a bereavement they 'put the lid on' their feelings, maintaining 'a stiff upper lip'. Their unresolved grief is triggered by being with grieving friends and is very threatening and painful.

Some dear friends may be hurting so deeply themselves about their own loss that they feel they cannot support the partner of the one who has died. If only they knew how supportive it is to have someone share your pain, to have them cry with you over the loss of that dear one. It is not 'dumping' their grief on to you. It is a deep sharing. How much more painful it is when those precious friends stay away. This was my experience with one in particular. David had been his closest friend and his death was a very great loss to his mate. I suspected that our friend was not making contact because his own pain was so great. His love for us would not allow him to, as he saw it, inflict anything more on us, least of all his pain. How I longed to see this precious soul, to share our common grief.

If by chance the reader feels as our friend did, my cry is, 'Don't stay away! Go as quickly as you can to cry with your friend. Scream and shout as well if you need to.'

For these reasons, and probably more, our experience of grief is very isolating. How much more important it is **for us**, as grieving parents, to be able to share it with our little ones rather than increase our sense of isolation by not doing so. Surely we do not want also to be cut off from our children in our pain?

Recently I met someone who was about to face the first family Christmas without Grandmother who had died two or three months earlier. This woman, with young adult children, was unable to find the energy and interest to do her Christmas shopping, and she suspected the others in the family felt the same. They were all trying to push themselves into creating a happy Christmas. When I asked her if they had shared their feelings about the coming Christmas celebrations, her blunt, 'O no!' closed the door to further discussion.

There are some people who are not yet ready to be open to other ways of dealing with their situation. They will not read this book. By the very fact that you have opened the book, **you** have signalled that you are ready to work creatively with the painful circumstances in which you now find yourself. I make no apologies for having no soft options to offer you!

It is a difficult, lonely, painful journey. Do not make it even more so by isolating yourself in this experience from your children. For as well as the children benefiting from this sharing, you will also discover what incredible strength these precious souls have to support you in this process.

# 3 'Be real!'

In accordance with our strong belief about being open and honest with the children, I have never concealed from them my own grief. They have been with me as I, have wept, they have seen my fury, they have heard my exclamations of disbelief.

Some of the precious memories of the days immediately following David's death are of Evania's beautiful presence supporting me as I wept an ocean of tears. Her hand on my head or shoulder had the strength of an adult's and her unspoken message to me was 'That's right, cry and cry and cry, for as long and as much as you need to.' There was a complete absence of fear or confusion for her in that. Her mother was being real and doing what, as we sensed from Evania's point of view, was natural and right.

There were occasions when I felt that the children may have been uncertain about the cause of my rage, tears, lack of energy, distracted behaviour. At such times I explained to them that my feelings were not related to them, rather to 'my sadness about Daddy...my anger towards him for leaving us ...' or 'I'm sorry, I forgot to get what you asked for because I was distracted by my thoughts about Daddy's accident.'

It is important that children do not feel that they are responsible for a parent's tears or anger, for then will fester and grow the most destructive of all feelings—guilt.

There were many, many times when I shouted at the children for no apparent reason. After the explosion I would draw them to me with a hug, 'O darlings, I'm sorry. I'm really not angry with you. Everything feels overwhelming at the moment and I'm not managing at all well. It's definitely not your fault.'

In fact the children did not seem to be at all disturbed by these explosions. I suspect that they sensed the source of that behaviour, just as Evania had done about my earlier tears. Still I felt it important to confirm their intuitions in order that there be no opportunity for guilt to walk into their lives.

Guilt and fear are, I believe, the most destructive of all the burdens we carry. The two usually form a partnership. Again it is most profoundly experienced in relation to such traumas as the separation of parents, death of a loved one, and illness. The child's thoughts go something like this: 'I was naughty and now Daddy has gone away. It must have been because I was naughty.'; 'I was naughty and made my mother sick.'

One of my most powerful experiences of childhood guilt remained with me for about thirty-five years, without my awareness of its existence. I was about three years old at the time of this experience. My mother had had one or more miscarriages. There is apparently no way that this could have been communicated to me directly. I understand that even my father had no knowledge of them until much later.

For some reason I believed that I was the cause of these miscarriages. Perhaps I had heard my mother say that she was unable to have the rest she needed because she had me to care for. In whatever way it happened, I took on the responsibility for the death of at least this one baby. I took my doll to the back of the garden and left her there so that the fairies could care for her. After all, how could I care for my baby when I had somehow mysteriously caused the death of my mother's baby.

I have not the slightest doubt that this was at least a contributing factor to my initial inability to have children. I had even convinced myself that I did not want children. I distanced myself from children. The possibility of enjoying them was too threatening: I might want children of my own, and **that** was impossible.

In my fortieth year the memory of the little girl giving her doll to the fairies came to me like a vision. Soon after weeping my way through that memory, Evania was conceived. What happened to my apparent infertility? Could it have been a product of my guilt?

Guilt is something which adults usually experience at some stage of their grief process. This is a natural part of the process and usually moves as we work through it. What I am talking about in relation to children is the guilt which remains, and which often buries itself deep in the unconscious. I urge you here to be aware of the risk of guilt in your little ones and to reduce that risk as far as is possible. Open and honest communication is, once again, 'the name of the game'!

My belief and experience is that children are comfortable, secure, accepting, at peace with adults who are being true to their own experience, **whatever** that might be. In contrast, children feel insecure, confused, anxious with adults who are trying to conceal their feelings, who are not being real. This relates as clearly to everyday life as to major events in our lives. A child will feel more secure in the presence of an adult who expresses sadness and rage, as well as joy, than someone who hides their tears or sits on their rage, allowing the child to see only the so-called positive feelings.

We had a beautiful example of this yesterday. A friend, who has been looking after the children while I write, began to talk about some of her own grief. She was holding Ketorah as she talked and then wept. Rather than the weeping disturbing Ketorah, she simply snuggled into our friend and went peacefully to sleep.

I want to stand on the verandah and shout to the mountains, to you all:

> BE REAL! BE REAL! Above all else BE REAL! And if you don't know how to be, then seek out someone who can help you get more in touch with yourself so that you **can** be real.

# 4 'Are you missing Daddy?'

In the first ten days or so after David's death there was much activity here. His sister Janice flew out from England, our dear friend Juno came down from the north coast to be with us, and there were other friends here for much of the time. Seemingly endless phone calls had to be made and received, and the funeral arranged.

The latter required much time and energy, as I was not prepared to hand everything over to a funeral director. I knew that it was important that I be as involved as possible and to this end I thought through every detail, taking my time to do so. As a result, the funeral did not take place until the eighth day after the accident.

With all this, to say nothing of the emotion charging our environment, it was easy not to notice otherwise seemingly insignificant signs of Evania's grief. As early as that first week, I learned some of those signs. It was yet something else altogether to always be aware of them, and indeed still is.

The cues from Evania were such everyday behaviour as complaining and restlessness. Nothing very obvious, certainly not dramatic. but it was not everyday behaviour for Evania. Each time I became aware of it and, more importantly, of its significance, I cuddled Evania and said something as simple as, 'Are you missing Daddy?' Her response was to snuggle into me for a minute or two before climbing down and getting on with her play, the grizzles and related behaviour having disappeared.

When I failed to be aware of Evania's grief behaviour, it continued without relief and with increasing intensity until we were all going crazy, or I recognised what was happening and responded appropriately. How simple it was at that time to support this little one in her grief—two or three minutes, a cuddle and simple acknowledgement of her grief. So simple, and so very important for her.

As is so often the case in all areas of our lives, the simple things are also the most profound, the most nourishing, the most healing—the comfort of another's touch, the wordless presence of someone who is truly 'there' for us, the unashamed tears of the one who weeps with us, the brief note which says, 'I love you'.

The stiff upper lip, denial of our feelings, fear of the other's expression of grief, withdrawal from the grieving one, 'giving her a good time', do not contribute to healing and restoration, are anything but nourishing, are insensitive and unreal.

What I am urging you to explore at this point is supportive behaviour, which would come naturally to us if we were not so burdened by our unhealthy conditioning about death. Before you give into the natural feelings of helplessness, perhaps even despair, look for the simple things you might do to support your child in his or her grief.

It is important, I believe, to give the little ones access to photos of the parent who has died. Evania carried photos of David around with her in those early days until, through so much handling, they became unrecognisable. They were then replaced with more until I put her favourite photo in a frame to give it a little more protection. I have since discovered the laminating process, by far the best way to have more durable photos which are easy to carry about.

Our dear friend Juno made a collage of photos related to David's life and it was the feature at home on the day of the funeral. I took photos of the collage and had them enlarged. The resulting poster, which I put on the wall at Evania's level, was also the object of much of her attention: simple and yet so meaningful to her.

For months after David died, Evania carried about various items of his clothing—slippers, socks, handker-chiefs. She also wore his sweatbands and played with his car keys. Clearly it was comforting for her to have these things about the house. She also took delight in seeing me in some of David's clothes. Even our beloved dog, Caleb, who had adored David, seemed to be comforted by carrying around one of David's shoes or boots!

It saddens me to hear of others who are bereaved ur-gently clearing away such evidence of the dead dear one's physical existence. At no time since David's death have I felt any need to dispose of all his things. There is no doubt that in those early days the presence of David's belongings, and Evania's access to them, was a very important part of her grief process. It was another simple source of comfort which would have been denied her had I obsessively cleared everything away.

Shortly before he died, David had made a swing for Evania. It was hung from the roof of our verandah and during the first week Evania spent many hours in it. She never tired of being pushed in the swing and we all commented on the comfort it seemed to offer her.

It is important that children be able to maintain contact with significant people in their lives, no matter how busy and distracted we might be. In our situation this was particularly important in relation to David's older two children who live with their mother, David's ex-wife. Before David died, the older girls spent weekends with us, Thursdays after school and more time during school holidays. We were not without difficulties about access from time to time and one of the first things I clarified with their mother on the day of David's death was that we would continue to see Gayle and Jasmin as often as we had prior to that day. Had this not been possible, we would have experienced a triple loss. It was comforting for us all to be together, particularly so for Evania.

Be aware of relationships the children have which may be in danger of coming to an unclear end if the people concerned were more your partner's friends or family, or people for whom you may not have cared very much. If they have been significant to the children, careful thought needs to be given to those relationships.

# 5 'Where is Daddy now?'

What wonderful teachers very young children are, if we would only be open to learning from them, precious souls, uncluttered by preconceptions and conditioning.

One of the precious experiences of those early days was again provided by our two-year-old. We took the children to say goodbye to the body in which their Daddy's spirit had lived during this life. Initially, when I lifted Evania up to see him, she was quiet and thoughtful. In the two hours we were there, she asked a number of times to be lifted up, or climbed on to a chair to see more clearly. Finally she climbed on to the chair for the last time, looked at David's body, shook her head and said, 'Daddy not here', climbed down and from then on showed no further interest in the proceedings.

She was right. David was not there. His discarded body was there and his presence, his spirit, was at home, as we all experienced. Sometimes Evania 'saw' him. She would call to us, 'Daddy there!' and point into the trees surrounding our house.

Evania's perception of David's death continued to comfort me. At the crematorium the casket was open and our friends were invited to say goodbye to David in whatever way felt right for them. Some had written poetry and placed that in the casket, others lay flowers there, or symbols of their relationship with David. During that hour Evania asked several times to be lifted up to see David. On the last occasion she spontaneously waved to him. 'Are you saying goodbye to Daddy?' I asked. She nodded, climbed down and again showed no further interest in what was happening.

Children know, in most instances, what they need to do if we give them the opportunity.

It is most important that children be allowed to see the body of the loved one as soon as possible after the death, for as long and as frequently as needed. Contrary to the expectations of many people, it is not a traumatic experience for them—unless traumatised adults put their expectations and distorted reality on to the children.

This was confirmed for me in Evania's experience. In seeing David's body, she recognised that his essence was no longer in that body and it was an important part of her process. It also gave her the opportunity to say goodbye, to complete that level of her relationship with her father. Her relationship with him continues. It is different. It is at a deeper level and the physical body is no longer part of that relationship.

We must take our cues from the children. They will show us what they need. Another child may need to spend much more time with a parent's body, yet another less time. As Evania gave us very clear cues, so also will your little one, if you do not get in the way. Trust the child's 'knowing', allow yourself to learn from her or him, trust yourself to respond appropriately.

This last point is perhaps the most difficult of all. Most of us have been conditioned, programmed, indoctrinated by our society's unhealthy attitudes to death. We have lost touch with what our deeper selves know to be true, real, natural in such a situation. The truth is that we do know at some level what that is. We can be helped by our children, bless their souls, to get in touch with that and in so doing, know how to respond appropriately. So trust your children. Learn from them. Allow them to help you get in touch with your own knowing. Trust your own knowing, not the cautious, fearful words from the voice of conditioning.

\*     \*     \*

Part of giving the children every opportunity to process their grief in whatever way they needed to was to take them to the wrecker's yard to see David's car. We had talked about the accident and could now see more clearly what had happened...

David had left home that morning to go to work just before seven. We had a landscaping business and David was on his way to pick up Jim, our partner. As he turned into the Great Western Highway, a car travelling up the highway struck his car full in the driver's door. There are questions about the accident which will forever remain unanswered, such as why did David not see the other car approaching? Perhaps the misty morning and the dark colour of the other car were contributing factors. Perhaps David's foot slipped from the brake to the accelerator. Was the other car travelling faster than David had judged? Who knows?

By seeing the car at the wrecker's yard, we could, however, understand clearly the result of the accident, how the driver's door had been pushed right into the centre of the car and how David could have had no chance of survival. He died instantly from a broken neck.

We took photos, as we had of David's body.

I am aware that many people will still be horrified by

all this. Their horror stems from their conditioning about death, not the reality of a child's response to the situation. If only they could step aside from their fears long enough to stand beside the little person at such a time, sensing their groundedness. It is a powerfully moving experience. Evania was thoughtful and asked some questions. At no time was there the slightest sign of discomfort, much less distress.

In the months that followed, Evania was able to talk about the accident more meaningfully, having seen the concrete evidence. She could play it out and work through it in play and sandplay therapy, which will be discussed later. The photos are important for Ketorah who has no conscious memory of all that. As her understanding develops and she asks questions, she will be able to see from the photos what we saw in those days.

It was another aspect of giving the children as much information as we had, from which they could select what was needed from them at the time, and since. And of course they will select different bits from this filing cabinet of information as the years pass and their understanding grows and changes. Different issues about David's death will present themselves for yet many years. There will be numerous questions. Some will be those all too many adults would not be able to answer, due to their own fear, their own unresolved issues about death.

To find answers to some of these questions for myself, and for the children later on, I undertook something of a pilgrimage some months after David died. It involved trips to 'behind the scenes' at the mortuary, the funeral home and the crematorium. Rather than being macabre, the experience was a tearing away of all the mystery surrounding such places, leaving a clean, clear, straight-forward process.

Why are such places traditionally shrouded in mystery? Why was it so difficult for the staff at the hospital to deal with my request to go to the mortuary? All my questions were answered so easily in going to these places, questions which seem so insignificant, unimportant, and yet which often present themselves frequently to the bereaved during endless sleepless nights.

They were answered for me then. Later, when the children ask questions, I will be able to answer them directly and clearly. Perhaps they will one day want to see these places for themselves and I will feel very comfortable about taking them.

For you there may be other unanswered questions, other issues. Today I was speaking to a friend who is also walking the path of deep grief. From a medical background, she has different unanswered questions for which it is proving even more difficult to find answers. The mystery and lack of openness and honesty about what should be a natural part of our lives is indeed reprehensible.

If our society were comfortable about death, if, as in certain other societies, death were as accepted as eating and sleeping, these questions would not need to be answered. We would know about those details as we learned to walk, talk and be socialised. Children would be involved with those who are dying, as naturally and easily as they stand beside Grandpa as he feeds his fish, or with Gran as she waters her garden or baths the dog. We would learn these things from adults as simply as Grandpa explains about the trout in his creek, or why he snores, or answers questions about whether or not the moon goes to sleep!

The reality is, of course, that our society does not make this learning easy for us. Consequently, it requires a great deal of effort from us to correct that tragedy of uninvolvement, the conspiracy of silence. There is, unfortunately, no other way for those of us who long for wholeness from our experience.

At a time when we are in such pain we should not have to fight the 'authorities' for information, battle with them to see the places where our loved one's body lay, or to have access to the ones who handled that dear body after death. But we do fight and by so doing we hope we are paving the way for others who follow us.

We can certainly make it easier for our own children, answering their questions simply and directly, making available to them all the information from which they take what they need. If it is not enough, they will ask further questions. If it is enough, they will take what they want from it, satisfied for the moment.

As we are open and honest with the children, they will feel freer to ask more questions. They will at times ask questions which we are unable to answer. My children often do. The reality is, of course, that no one has the answers to everything. Some parents and other adults try to deny that reality to the children, perhaps out of a sense of helplessness, their own anxiety or insecurity. Rather than fearing or being embarrassed by the gaps in our knowledge and understanding, we need to feel comfortable about them, welcome them rather than deny them, be defensive or fight against them.

Not only is it a fact that we do not have all the answers,

it is healthy and indeed creative to have these 'I don't know' spaces in our lives. It is in the 'I don't know' spaces that we explore and discover new territories in the mind, emotions, spirit and body.

> Can I reach that high shelf? I don't know.
> Perhaps if I move my hips this way and my chest and shoulders this way...
> Ah, there, now I can reach it!

Similarly with our emotions...

> Why am I feeling so irrationally angry? I don't know. What triggered it? Is it always triggered by the same thing? When and where was there such a trigger early in my life?

Through such exploration we can discover that the anger is not related to the present at all, rather to something in our distant past, and we are better able to place the anger where it belongs, in the past.

In relation to death and life after death...

> Where is David now? I don't know. If I am open to discoveries in this area I am sure that they will become apparent.

When the children ask questions which you are unable to answer, be honest with them about that.

> 'Where is Daddy now?'
> 'I don't know, darling. I also would like to know the answer to that question. Perhaps we will discover it one day. We can explore the question

together, for there is an answer somewhere. We know that there are some beautiful lizards in our bush though we are not always able to find them. Though they are hidden for long periods, we know they are still there somewhere. It is like that with answers to our questions.

They are there somewhere, and if we keep our ears and eyes open we will one day discover the answer, or at least something which helps us to understand more about the question.'

# 6 'Thank you for your love...'

I never cease to be shocked and horrified when I hear
people relate their own experience of bereavement at a
very early age. So often, it seems, the dead loved one is
never spoken of. It is as though he or she had never
existed.

I cannot relate to that in any way at all. How much more
difficult it must be for very young children who remain in
touch with the reality of the loved one's continuing existence on a spiritual or soul level.

Evania was perhaps closer to David during his life here
than any of us. It would be unthinkable to deny that reality.
How confusing, damaging, wounding, tragic that would be
for her. Much of Evania's spiritual and emotional development is a result of the bonding with her father. That bond
can never be broken. It **is**, no matter what happens.

We acknowledge this by talking about David and the
things we did together, by poring over the many photos we
have, singing the songs he loved, and dancing as David did
so often.

We created a little memorial garden in a quiet part of
the property, where we can go to remember David and be
with him in a particular way. Of course we can be with
him in a spiritual sense at any moment and in any place,
just as we can pray or meditate driving the car, washing
the dishes or walking in the bush. As with prayer and
meditation, however, it is helpful to have special times and
special places, to create little chapels for that purpose.

As I write this, Evania has just been down to a tree which was planted over the place where our dog, Cindy, was buried a few months before David's death. Evania had quite spontaneously made some little treasures from clay to put under Cindy's tree. It was another little part of her process about death.

Our relationships remain with those who have left this earth as surely as they continue when we are separated during daily life, when a parent goes to work and the children are at home. The bond exists into eternity.

Our beloved Geoff, who has committed himself to us in a full-time relationship, will shortly be joining us here. I have found the children's relationships with him to be deeply moving and I am in awe of their beauty. Geoff will never, I trust, be threatened by Evania's and Ketorah's relationships with David, who will always be their Daddy.

I have heard someone speaking of two children whose father had died and their mother was marrying again. It was said that these girls now had 'a new Daddy'. It is true that Geoff will be a wonderful father to Evania and Ketorah, **but** David will always be their Daddy, their relationship with him ongoing.

Our girls may one day decide to call Geoff 'Daddy'. If they do, Geoff and I, as we continue to support them in their relationship with David, will see that there is no confusion between David's relationship with them, and Geoff's.

\* \* \*

My greatest trauma associated with death was when, at the age of three or four, my great-grandfather died. The pain and confusion associated with that remained with me into adulthood. No one recognised the importance of my relationship with Great-grandpa who was to me the most loving person in my life. To the rest of the family he was mean and selfish, totally without love.

I have no doubt that he had done all the things they spoke about. But it was not true for me. For me he was none of those things. I felt so alone, left by him, and our loving relationship denied completely by those around me.

Shortly after David died, I wrote to my beloved great-grandpa.

> Dear Grandpa,
> Here at last is the letter I should have written to you ages ago. I do so much want to tell you how I feel about you and to say the goodbye that was not said when you died. I want to tell you that you were the only person in my childhood who I felt really loved me. In fact, not only in my childhood, rather well into my thirties.
>
> The difficult thing for me is that all my life I have heard nothing but criticism of you from the rest of the family. All I have heard about is what a most dreadful person you were. Grandpa, it hurts me deeply to hear them speak like this of you. They seem unable to even hear me when I tell them about my experience of you.
>
> I remember you taking me for walks, holding my hand as we walked down Vine Lane. I remember the dog chasing a cat there, that is until the cat stopped running and turned to face the dog, which in turn screamed to an ungainly halt!
>
> More than that, I have very little memory of

you, except the sense of this beautiful love, yours for me.

I was four when you died. You died at our house and, despite all that the family say to the contrary, I remember going into your room at, or very soon after, the time of your death. I do not remember how I felt then.

It does not matter what the family say about you. You were, for me, love. Maybe in the simplicity of that little four-year-old was the wisdom which saw the real, true you, your inner beauty.

I feel very close to you as I write this, as though you are very much here with me. It's been a long time since we were together, thirty-seven years. How lovely it is to talk to you now.

Grandpa, I want to thank you for the love you gave me.

It has just occurred to me that it must have been soon after your death that my physical disability became evident. Is there some relationship between these events, the loss of your love and my complete immobility? Mm, it is interesting!

Part of my reason for writing to you was to say goodbye and now it seems more like a reunion, a re-establishment of the relationship. I suppose the four-year-old is saying goodbye and the fourty-one-year-old is meeting you again.

Well, Grandpa, there doesn't seem to be anything more to say at the moment. It's been lovely

talking to you and, contrary to my expectations
(I have problems with having too many expectations!), it has been a very gentle time.

Goodbye Grandpa.

> Much love,
> Heather.

Writing this letter was a profound experience through
which came healing. I re-established contact with my
great-grandfather and since then have received strength
and comfort from that relationship.

All those years of pain and confusion could have been
avoided had there been an aware adult there for me at the
time of his death.

A further tragedy in our society is the failure to acknowledge the bonds we have with those who died without our
ever having known them. This became very clear to me
one day when I was greatly distressed by Evania's grief.
In a moment of desperation I sensed the presence of
David's father who had died several years before I met
David. As I responded to Grandpa David's presence, I
asked him to comfort his little grand-daughter in her pain.

Later I wrote to him:

Dear David (Senior),

I want to write to you because I felt so close to
you today. It seemed that you were with us,
supporting, loving your little grand-daughter in
her agony.

I sense you as a very loving grandfather to my
little ones, and that is indeed precious to me.

Isn't it strange that we say things like, 'They
have only one grandfather, their other grandfa-

ther is dead.' What a denial of your existence, of your existence on this earth during the time of your life here and your very present existence now at a deep spiritual level.

How thankful I am to have you as the grandfather of my little ones, and indeed as my father too, through my relationship with David. How thankful I am to have become aware of your presence, of your comfort, encouragement, love.

I hear about you from Alice, how you met, your life together, your affectionate nature. I can see my precious little Evania and Ketorah snuggling into you! I can see you comforting Evania in her grief. How she needs the comfort of her grandfather now. How she needs to experience the warmth and strength of those wonderful arms of her Grandfather David. You can tell her about her Daddy as he was, as your son. You can explain to her where he is now. I can see her looking into your face with her big wide-open eyes, listening attentively to your words about her Daddy. She is understanding in a new way, at a deeper level, so that she is now more able to let go of the physical Daddy.

'Bampa David, where is my Daddy? Why doesn't he come see me?'

You are able to answer all the questions that I find so difficult, for a Grandpa has such wisdom, especially one who has passed through death into glory, light, peace, truth.

So, dearest 'Bampa David', who I have only just met, thank you for being present to us. Thank you for helping me to be aware of your presence, and all that you are for us. Thank you for your blessing on us, especially on Evania. Make known your presence to her. I will talk to her about you so that she can know her other Grandpa, her dearest 'Bampa David'.

It horrifies me to think that I, along with millions of others in this life, have denied the existence of loved ones who have died. Denied their existence by not making them known to those who didn't know them during their life here. How incredible that is, especially for one who thought she believed in 'the Communion of Saints'!

What a blessing that there is now light!

My love to you David/Bampa,

Heather.

I talked to Evania about Grandpa David. David's mother, Alice, was at the time visiting us from England and I encouraged her to talk to the girls about their grandfather. It was a strengthening and healing time for us all.

It is another loss for children in our society, who are denied the reinforcement of the spiritual bonds they have with other members of the family who have died before they were born. If we were to acknowledge those bonds when the children are very young and still in touch with the reality of the existence of those loved ones, on a spiritual plane, less damage would be done by the attitudes of our society. I am sure that they would then, and for the rest of their lives, draw strength, wisdom, comfort from the reality of those bonds.

In the Christian Church the 'Communion of Saints' is declared as part of the Creed. That concept has a deeper reality for me now. That reality is there in my children, naturally, and I pray that they will not lose it as I did.

# 7 'Good-bye Caleb'

For children as young as Evania, other events which result in the same feeling—in this case loss and sadness—become one for the child.

Eight months after David died, we moved to Adelaide to be near my family. We took our beloved dog, Caleb. Caleb is an enormous dog and young, with boundless energy. He did not adjust to suburban life and we eventually found a wonderful home for him with a country family.

The loss of our much-loved Caleb was for Evania a very strong trigger related to David's death as well. The two experiences became one. Caleb and Daddy were mentioned in the same breath.

Of course I had prepared the children for Caleb's departure, explaining the reasons for it. I told them that we would find some people who would love and care for him. 'And cuddle him?' was Evania's response. We were all there when Elizabeth and Brian first came to see Caleb. They assured Evania that they would cuddle him and she seemed satisfied, as I am sure she was.

There was no apparent reaction from the children in the first few weeks after Caleb left. I missed him more than the children seemed to. Then Evania began to ask for him, crying that she missed him. So one Saturday we set off for Clare which is about three hours' drive north of Adelaide. On the way we bought Caleb a lovely big bone at Evania's suggestion.

As we drew close to our destination Evania became very distressed and vomited. While at Caleb's new home she cried inconsolably, with our dear Caleb trying to comfort her. Even the gift of the bone was no longer of any interest to Evania. Our new friends were unbelievably sensitive and caring and very supportive in this, a most painful time for us all. Nothing brought any comfort to Evania. We all sensed that she needed to sob her little heart out and supported her as she did so. I think this was for me the most difficult of all our painful experiences. I wrote in my journal: 'If it had not been for appreciating the enormous significance of Evania seeing Caleb, I would not have been able to cope at all. As it was, it was with great difficulty.'

After an hour and a half we left and drove back to Adelaide. Evania was uncharacteristically silent on the way back. In fact, for a period of four hours she had not spoken. She was either completely silent or crying; for half an hour she slept. The crying began again when we arrived home. I put her straight to bed. The next day she was 'as bright as a button'.

I had taken some beautiful photos of Caleb while visiting him that day. I promptly had the film developed and made a collage of these and earlier photos of him, some of which included David. Both children referred to the poster several times a day in the following week.

We visited Caleb the following weekend and the experience could not have been more different to that of the previous week. Evania was very relaxed, cuddled her precious Caleb and played happily in the garden, with Caleb moving in and out of her play. This time Evania ceremoniously presented a large fresh bone to her loving mate.

It was a day of great joy for me. How precious it was to see and sense the progress Evania had made in only one week. I knew that what was happening for her in relation to Caleb was also occurring for her in the process related to David's death. As she worked through her grief about Caleb, more was being resolved for her about the loss of her father.

I was tempted, you can be sure, to get another animal, something to relieve her grief. Had I done so, Evania would have been denied the opportunity to work through her grief in the way she did at that time. I had to allow myself to be in pain, watching this heart-broken little girl in hers. By supporting her in it and not attempting to ease her pain, and therefore my own, we were both able to move forward in our respective processes.

A similar experience occurred sometime after the loss of Caleb. Evania saw a sparrow run over by a car when we were out shopping one day. The death of that little bird was another trigger for her grief. Daddy and the bird were one. The two accidents, the two deaths, were one. Evania was still inconsolable hours later.

I went to our sandplay room (more of that later), selected a bird, a daddy figure, a smashed car, an ambulance and another car. Using these symbols, I played out David's accident, and the bird's death, on the living-room floor. Evania quickly took over and played out the two incidents over and over again. Initially the intensity of the play was dramatic. With each repetition of the two accidents, that intensity lessened slightly. Finally, after almost an hour, the energy had dissipated altogether and Evania's interest was elsewhere. She had worked through another part of her process.

'The bird and Daddy' remained with Evania for some weeks, with her always referring to them as one. The bird used in the play therapy that day, was cuddled and stroked for at least some part of each day. For the remainder of the time it lived on our little altar or shrine.

Finally Evania gave the bird to a particularly dear friend when he was visiting us. He was instructed to take the bird home and care for it. It was a sign of more letting go, or completion of that 'bit' for our courageous (now) three-year-old.

A few weeks later, Evania came running in from the garden, calling to us with great excitement. She had found a dead bird on the path. We all went outside and, again taking our cues from Evania, supported her in wrapping the bird in a paper napkin, carefully laying it in a hole dug for it, covering it and placing flowers and rice on the little bird's grave.

Had I been more aware at the time of the first bird's death, I could have gathered up the little body and taken it home. Evania could have cared for it and performed her little ritual around it. If I had done that, she may have worked through that incident and the associated grief related to David more quickly and less painfully. I was not aware then, and Evania found that opportunity a few weeks later, by which time I was more aware and could support her in it.

Of course many children perform such rituals around pets and other creatures which have breathed their last. That is as it should be. Many adults fail to be aware of how very important these little incidents and their accompanying rituals are in the child's attitude to, and working through of, issues about death.

Such incidents allow death to be for the children the reality it is. They allow death to be a natural normal part of life without the mystery and fear so many of us carry in relation to it.

In my own childhood death was never spoken of. When pets died, they were whisked away, never to be seen by us, and that pet replaced immediately with another so that we would not be upset.

I have had many pets both in my childhood and as an adult. Four months before David died, my dearest dog, Cindy, was hit by a car on the country road outside our home. She died instantly. With David's support, at the age of forty-one I experienced for the first time what it was to stroke a dead pet, to talk to it, to be involved in burying it and to weep beside the grave.

I had not recognised until then how much fear I had in relation to death. And it was a result of it all being such a mystery. As I approached Cindy's lifeless body, it was the most natural thing in the world to caress her, talk to her, and to supervise David in the burying of her.

While writing this I have been remembering the weeks of tears which followed Cindy's death. There seemed at the time to be a bottomless lake of tears. I now realise that the tears were not only for Cindy. They were for all the pets in my life for which I had never grieved. There was never time to grieve, for the lost pet was immediately replaced with a lovable, warm, bouncing bundle of a puppy or a fluffy, playful kitten, which then became the focus of attention and source of much joy. And the grief was sent diving into the unconscious to remain unacknowledged and unresolved, to be added to when the next pet died ... and the next.

Even in adult life I had continued the pattern of my family in replacing the dead pet as soon as possible in order to relieve the pain.

In her death, Cindy gave me her greatest gift and David was the one there to support me in the process. Four months later, when David died, I was so much clearer than I would otherwise have been.

Today we visited a friend whose elderly cat is dying. As I stood beside him I was deeply moved by his 'presence'. He was in no distress and there was a wonderful gentleness and strength in this noble creature who, we sensed, knew he was dying.

How insane we are to 'put down' animals who are old or ill. This practice is yet another of the symptoms of our dis-ease in relation to death.

What a gift it was for me to be there with that dying cat, to sense his serenity and acceptance as he waited... surrounded by the love of his family with whom he had spent his fourteen years. Evania and Ketorah also met Bearkins in the last few days of his life. We explained that he was old, his body worn out and soon his spirit would leave his body—he would die.

A few mornings later the phone rang. Bearkins, we learned, had died a little while earlier. We went to see his body. Thanks to the love and sensitivity of our dear friend who invited us to come and see Bearkins that day, the children (and I) were able to be involved in his dying and death. The children each did a drawing and picked some flowers, all of which they laid carefully and lovingly around Bearkins in his box. We stroked him and said goodbye to this lovely old cat who now, with the struggle of living gone, looked so young.

How important it is that we do not deny ourselves and our children such opportunities by handing over to the vet or to someone else the responsibility of our pets.

Support and encourage your children in their little rituals, allow them to be involved in the dying and death of their pets. In fact, take your cues from them and they will receive what they need in the situation.

The more I share such profound experiences the more aware I become of a sense of deep loss through not having been open to such opportunities earlier in my life. I have that same sense of loss in relation to our society in general, and individuals in particular, denied such depths of experience in their living as a result of attitudes about dying.

# 8 Evania Doll: play therapy and sandplay

I have spoken about the use of play therapy in relation to Evania's distress over the death of the bird. Here is another example of the way in which a simple process can have a powerful effect.

Just over twelve months after David died, Evania woke crying from an afternoon sleep. I asked her if she had had a dream. 'No' was her response. She remained distressed during the afternoon until during the evening meal she said to me, 'You not knock Daddy over again, will you?' In response to my questions and comments, Evania related her dream:

> 'My mother knocked Daddy over and the chair too... naughty, naughty. You do it again and I'll smack your bottom. You not knock Daddy over again?'

At the time I did not know what to do with the dream. In the following weeks Evania was unwell. 'A virus,' the doctor said. She was fretful, waking up crying and saying she wanted Daddy, day and night.

I was beside myself, feeling inadequate, helpless and very frustrated. Evania had become uncharacteristically defiant as well. I wondered if she no longer felt supported, understood in her grief. As a result of the dream, I wondered if she blamed me for David's death. There was certainly some anger towards me about something.

Eventually we had a play therapy session one evening before bed. We used four characters, each represented by a doll or teddybear. The characters were Mother Ted, Father Ted, Evania Doll and Ketorah Doll.

I began by asking Evania what Evania Doll was doing. The play continued...

> Evania Doll landed heavily on Mother Ted's head. I exclaimed on behalf of Mother Ted, 'Oo, you're hurting me, Evania Doll!'
>
> Evania then used Evania Doll to beat Mother Ted, following which she picked up Mother Ted and threw it to the other side of the room.
>
> I commented about Evania Doll being angry with Mother Ted.
>
> Evania Doll then kissed Father Ted several times. Evania asked me to kiss Father Ted, which I did.
>
> Evania retrieved Mother Ted and laid it on the floor, explaining, 'She tired.'
>
> Then all the characters were arranged on the floor together. 'Going to bed,' Evania explained.
>
> Evania finally lay on the floor herself and cuddled Mother Ted.
>
> The energy seemed to have dissipated and the session ended.

Evania went to bed for the first time for weeks without any fuss and gave me a lovely warm 'giving' cuddle. I asked her if she still felt angry with me and she shook her head.

It still amazes me that such a simple process of half an

hour or so could have such powerful results.

As play is the child's natural medium of self-expression, it is perhaps the most obvious and appropriate tool to use in supporting children to work with difficult issues in their lives. I find that it is not always easy, even now, to remember that this most simple tool is often the most powerful. Of course many issues are resolved in the normal play of children, which is why play is so important in their development.

I earlier referred to our sandplay room. Sandplay is a non-verbal form of therapy which provides access to pre-verbal levels of the psyche, so is particularly useful in working with children.

It involves creating a three-dimensional picture in a box of sand. The picture is created from a selection of hundreds of miniature figures and symbols covering all areas of life. The pieces include people, animals and birds, cars, planes, boats, trees and flowers, rocks, stones, shells, seeds, buildings, musical instruments, fantasy characters, jewels, anything, in fact, which is small enough to be used in the sandbox, the dimensions of which make it possible for the child to see the whole box in one glance: about seventy by fifty-five by eight centimetres.

Sandplay is once again in the world of symbolism. Each piece represents a part of the psyche. The child or adult creating the picture is able to select whichever of the pieces in the collection catches the eye, and is then free to do anything at all within the boundaries of the sandplay box, in the secure, protected environment of the sandplay room.

In an awesome way, the very process of creating the picture in the sand moves material which lies buried in the unconscious, and those parts of the wounded psyche are healed.

Because the sandplay or picture represents aspects of the psyche, it is possible to see from the sandplay something of what is going on in the child's psyche and, where appropriate, take measures to support that particular part of the healing process.

Sandplay is a recognised tool in psychotherapy, particularly in relation to children. It is also helpful for adults who find verbal forms of therapy of limited use, or as one of a number of tools used alongside each other. I use sandplay as one of the tools in my own inner work and after David died did a sandplay at least once a week for many months.

Sandplay as we know it today was originally referred to as 'World Techniques'. Margaret Lowenfeld, who was the first therapist to use this form of therapy, was a Freudian psychiatrist working in London in the 1930s. Later, in the fifties, a Jungian analyst, Dora Kalff, after studying World Techniques in London, developed her own form of sandplay therapy in Switzerland. Both these therapists have written books on the subject. Estelle Weinrib, another Jungian analyst, has recently had published her excellent book on sandplay therapy. (Publishing details of these books and other reading material will be found in the appendix at the back of this book.)

The ways of using sandplay are as limitless as one's imagination, sensitivity and intuition in relation to the one doing the sandplay. In our own experience the sandplay can be either completely undirected or, where appropriate, varying degrees of direction or personal involvement in the sandplay offered.

With an adult who tends to operate very much from the mind and is out of touch with the feelings, I will usually minimise discussion about the sandplay, leaving the process of creating the sandplay to do its work. In such a situation, to offer direction during the sandplay or comments afterwards might support the person in remaining dependent on the use of the mind as the only way of dealing with life. As the person becomes more in touch with the feelings, it may be more appropriate to discuss the sandplay and perhaps give some direction or suggestions, one of which might be to have dialogue with the significant figure in the sandplay, perhaps the little girl who is alone in a corner of the picture. I will encourage the one doing the sandplay to talk to the little girl, or might myself ask the little figure questions which the one creating the sandplay will answer. We will very quickly make some important discoveries about the little girl who represents a part of that person's psyche. Soon some connections will be made between that little figure and the issue which is presently concerning the person doing the sandplay.

Children sometimes need some direction. We have been quite directive with Evania at times, taking specific pieces from the collection and setting up in the sandtray a scene which represents the issue of the day, perhaps something to do with family dynamics or David's accident. We will sometimes assume the character of one of the pieces, perhaps the figure Evania has buried in the sand. In this way it is very similar to the incidents I have mentioned in the section on play therapy. In playing out the issue, energy related to the difficulty moves and there is partial or often complete resolution.

It may be helpful to move a key piece in the sandplay someone has completed and ask how it feels to have it in the new position. Perhaps the child figure in the sandplay is a long way from the adult figure in the picture. The child who has created the sandplay may feel very uncomfortable about the figures of the child and adult being so close to each other. In the sandplay box this discomfort can be played out, ways of being closer explored and the feeling of distance resolved.

There are times when there is no direct involvement at all in the child's sandplay. In one instance a pre-school child had become very withdrawn, to the point of relating only to animals. She did three sandplays each a week apart. There was no direct involvement from any other person. At the end of the third sandplay she filled the sandplay box with all the snakes in the collection (snakes are a symbol of transformation), washed her hands and said that she did not want to come again. From that moment she was transformed: spontaneous, outgoing, relating to adults and children. If I had not seen it myself I would not have believed it.

At another time a little boy, soon to begin school, had been diagnosed as 'hyperactive'. Traditional medicine and alternative treatments had failed to help him. In the sandplay room there was no evidence in his behaviour of his hyperactivity. His face was alive, his eyes bright, his movements purposeful, clear and unhurried. There were noticeable changes in his behaviour after only one sandplay.

Young children usually tell the story as they are creating the picture, giving a commentary to themselves which is also invaluable to the understanding of the adult supporting the child in the process. Such a commentary can give a very clear picture of what is happening in the child's inner world. I sometimes have a cassette recorder operating to record the child's story as the sand picture is created. It is helpful to be able to listen to it again, picking up new clues and gaining new insights into the child's inner life.

As part of the recording of a sandplay and at least as important, acknowledging and honouring it, is a photograph taken of the completed sandplay. Children respond enthusiastically to having such a photograph and adults who have done a sandplay can take home a record of what they have done. By studying it during the succeeding weeks they can gain more insights into their own inner world.

I do not immediately dismantle a sandplay if it can be avoided, as it is helpful to spend more time with it, sensing more of what it is saying about the person's inner life. Notes are made about it which along with the photograph form a record. The movement or progress seen in such a series is at times almost unbelievable.

Obviously it takes time to gather a collection of sandplay pieces which fill a room as do ours. It does not take long, however, to gather enough useful pieces to make such an exercise possible and helpful to your little one. To begin with you can use a cardboard carton as the sandtray. Such figures as soldiers and animals, cars, trains, boats and planes are easily and inexpensively obtained from toy shops, supermarkets and garage sales. You and your little one can have fun collecting shells, seed pods, pebbles and other natural things for the collection. It is amazing how many useful pieces you will find around your home, discarded toys, ornaments, any small items used in daily life.

Once you begin the collection you will discover that friends have many unwanted pieces which to the sandplay collection are useful and indeed precious. It is easy to find bits of jewellery, beads, buttons, counters. Novelty key-rings are a source of interesting symbols. We have a pile of discarded key-ring fittings somewhere! Cake decorating shops are a rich source of sandplay pieces and we watch for such shops wherever we go. You can also make things yourself from clay or a similar substance, matchsticks, balsa wood, cardboard.

A word of warning! If you begin a sandplay collection, do not be surprised if you become addicted to seeking out pieces for your collection. It can become a fun-filled and harmless obsession. I suspect that there is a frustrated collector in all of us. How lovely to be able to put it to such good use!

If you do decide to follow up some of these ideas, it is important that the sandplay be regarded by the children as something quite special, rather than simply a few more toys to play with. The collection should be kept separate from other toys and be used only with adult supervision. It is after all a powerful and beautiful form of therapy and must be honoured as such and regarded with respect.

# 9 A candle for David: symbolism and ritual

I mentioned earlier our little altar or shrine. Ritual and symbolism are very important in the life of a child. They are, or should be, equally important for adults. Most of us, to our great deprivation, have lost touch with how deeply meaningful is the world of symbolism and the importance of ritual.

Our little altar is a special place where precious symbols are placed as an acknowledgement or honouring of the importance of that symbol in our lives. It may be a pine cone, as a symbol of new life, or a bird, as a symbol for Evania relating to David's death. Our altar may hold symbols associated with spiritual traditions. Sometimes I place one of my drawings there.

One of the symbols which has been important to me in the last few years is the butterfly, a symbol of transformation. That symbol held great power for me as I sensed a new 'me' emerging. And so anything with the butterfly symbol caught my eye, earrings, dress material, paintings, sculpture, wrapping paper. Another powerful symbol for me is the eagle. With its power, strength, ability to soar to great heights, its wonderful vision and its ability to be carried by the currents without any need to struggle, it speaks to me of what can be in my own life. I am reminded of the possibilities by having beautiful sculptures of eagles in brass, copper and ceramic in our home.

Our work in the world can be a conscious symbol of our own inner journey. Some years ago I experienced great comfort from restoring some brass in a church. It was an anonymous labour of love. I sat for hours in a hidden part of the church and worked away. The brass had been coated with a protective varnish, some of which had worn off, leaving badly tarnished areas. As I stripped the surface back to its original glory, it was a powerful symbol of what was happening in my own life, where there was a stripping away of the layers of conditioning, of old patterns of thinking and reacting, of old hurts. I trusted that one day the 'original' Heather would be revealed in her glory!

Similarly at that time I was restoring the beautifully carved timber in the church, all of which had layers and layers of wax and polish, such that the beautiful grain in the timber was no longer evident. What a long, tedious task it was. But it was so rewarding to see the timber come 'alive' again. More than that it was a nourishing symbol fo the same sort of process in my life. Similarly, my inner work is a long, tedious process. And the rewards are incalculable. As with the brass and the wood, if I look at the total project it becomes overwhelming. If I look at the small part on which I am working at the moment it is manageable, and I see daily the results of my work.

It is helpful to look at your child's behaviour in a symbolic sense as well. This behaviour can symbolise something deeper. An example of this with Evania occurred while we were in Brisbane a few months ago. Wherever we went, where we were staying and on campus where I was studying, Evania was asking others for food. When she eventually vomited one afternoon I knew that this behaviour required closer attention. Her body did not need extra nourishment, that was clear.

The next day I spoke to the group of trainees, explaining that Evania's request for food was symbolic of her much greater need for more emotional nourishment. Her way of expressing that need was to ask for physical nourishment. I suggested that, rather than respond to these requests, the members of the group give her something of themselves, not their food. More appropriate would be a cuddle, perhaps a short walk with her, sing Evania a song, dance with her or tell a story.

The response of the group was most encouraging. Many expressed appreciation for having been given some guidelines for their relating to Evania, whose real needs were now being met. Food ceased to be an issue.

\*   \*   \*

About the time of the first sparrow's death, I had bought some votive candles. These small candles are used in Catholic and some Anglican churches, and differently designed candles in Orthodox churches. A candle is lit for someone in need, in memory of a dear one, or in thanksgiving. The lighting of the candle is a symbol of the love and prayer of the person lighting it.

The candle itself is a symbol of light and life and I suspect that children know this intuitively. I also suspect that this is why so many of us love to have candles burning, even though electricity has determined that we no longer need them as a source of light. The lighted candle remains a wonderful symbol of the warmth and light and energy of our own lives, however conscious or unconscious we may be of those qualities in ourselves or in those around us.

One day when Evania was distressed about 'the bird

and Daddy', I asked her if she would like us to light a candle for them. Still crying, she nodded. I lit the candle and placed it where she could see it from her bed. Evania snuggled in under the bedclothes, watched the candle for a few minutes and went into a peaceful sleep, as the candle continued to burn for 'the bird and Daddy'.

Whatever your religious beliefs, or the absence of such beliefs, the meaningfulness of symbolism and ritual is an important aid to supporting your little children in their grief. It may or may not be meaningful to you. It most certainly is to your little one.

In the process of being open to your child's experience in this way, who knows, you may even discover that it is meaningful to you as well! What a wondrous bonus that would be! Your life will be inexpressibly richer if you allow the world of symbolism to take its rightful place.

\*　　\*　　\*

'I sad cos Daddy can't hear me.'

This was an issue for Evania for several days. She woke at night crying, 'Daddy can't hear me.' She cried during the day, 'Daddy can't hear me.' All my explanations and reassurances were totally meaningless to her. Eventually I tumbled on an idea which I expected to make some sense to Evania. It was in relation to our practise of sending letter-cassettes to David's mother and sister in England. 'When we speak to Grandma Alice and Auntie Janice on the cassette,' I suggested to Evania, 'we know that they will hear us, though we cannot see them. We tell them all about what we have been doing and how we're feeling, and they listen to the cassette with delight. They love to hear us tell them about all the things that are important to us.

And it's like that with Daddy. He can hear us even though we can't see him. He loves to hear you tell him about what's happening for you, how you are feeling and what you've been doing.'

When I saw that this explanation was making some connection with Evania, I asked her if she would like to speak to Daddy on the cassette. And so she did. She in fact said very little on the tape. That was not the issue. The important thing for her was that she now felt that she could talk to her Daddy and that he would hear her. That satisfied her need. When she had finished with the tape, we took it down to the post office and posted it to 'Daddy, c/o God'.

One of the things Evania does most often when she is feeling sad about David is a drawing for him. Again we complete the process by placing it in an envelope, addressing it, putting a stamp on it and posting it.

I know of a little girl whose mother died not long after David. I remember hearing that she had written a note to her mother and, rather than posting it, she put it in a bottle and sent it out to sea from the beach near her home. Another way of dispatching a drawing, note or gift, is by putting it in the fire and allowing the smoke to carry the message to its destination, or by writing the message on a balloon and watching it float up and out of sight.

As mentioned earlier, Evania's most recent little ritual is to make gifts out of clay. The offerings are placed under Cindy's tree or in David's garden to be carried away, washed into the earth by the rain.

The possibilities ar endless. As in our own lives, different symbols and rituals will be meaningful at different stages of the child's process.

I emphasise the importance of acknowledging, honouring these little rituals.  They will lose much of their healing power if our attitude to them is, 'O well, it keeps her amused...' or 'She likes to do it so I play along with her...' It is not simply amusing, it is not 'mere' play.  It is profoundly important to the process and must be honoured as such.

# 10  Ketorah crying: the very young baby

My writing to date has been in relation to our experience of Evania's grief and I have said very little, if anything, about Ketorah's process.  My emphasis has been on Evania because her grief has been more obvious.

Ketorah's process has been at a more unconscious level so far, though no less significant.  She was five months old when David died.  The bond between Ketorah and her father was very strong.  David had experienced profound healing and changes in himself as a result of Ketorah's presence during the pregnancy and especially at her birth. I sometimes wonder if that strong bond with David has contributed to her being so strong and secure.  Perhaps the fact that her relationship with David was not so much at a conscious level has enabled her to be less disrupted by the loss of the physical David.  Rather, she remains in touch with him, gaining strength and comfort from that spiritual relationship with him.

Those of us who remember David, who are struggling with the loss of the physical David, cannot help but have that loss detract somewhat from the spiritual relationship. It takes a long time and much work before we are able to let go of the physical David and connect completely with his essence.  Perhaps this is not so for Ketorah.

That is not to deny the reality of her own grief process. Evania, my little teacher, has helped me to recognise

Ketorah's grief. There were occasions, beginning about a year after David died, when Ketorah cried for long periods and for no apparent reason. After my fruitless attempts to discover what was upsetting her, Evania announced, 'Torah crying cos Daddy not coming.' Eventually I acted on Evania's knowledge and she was proven right. I acknowledged verbally to Ketorah her sadness about her Daddy, talked to her about him and his love for her, showed her photos of us all together.

Ketorah's response was dramatic. The sobbing eased, she became very attentive to what I was saying and the distraught baby, who earlier could not be comforted, became still and pensive for a time before running off to do whatever came next in her play.

There were times when Ketorah woke during the night, sobbing inconsolably. There is a particular cry which I now recognise as being grief (so also for Evania). At such times I held her and talked about David, acknowledged to her the sadness, and she relaxed and returned easily to sleep.

Since our return to the Mountains Ketorah has spoken daily of David. Perhaps it is because we are here in the place where he lived and died. Does she experience his presence here in a different way? Perhaps it is because her verbal skills are increasing. Perhaps it is because I am writing about these things and the children are at some level picking up the theme.

Six or eight months ago our dear friend Mike, who is also a brilliant therapist, wrote a beautiful letter to Evania. At the time she was finding it particularly difficult to let go of the physical David. When the letter arrived, and in the following weeks, Evania did not seem

to relate to it. Recently she has frequently asked me to
read it to her, until now it has become an almost nightly
event, following the other bed-time stories.

Evania's interest in the letter was at least matched by
Ketorah's. It seemed that, to the little sister, the content
of the letter was perhaps even more meaningful. The
letter:

Dear Evania,

Our love and blessings to you. Guess what? A
very beautiful fairy called Teala came to visit us.
You know she is a beautiful light fairy, all
dressed in blue, and sparkling. Her home is in
the stars, where people go to walk when they are
dreaming, or when their bodies die. Daddy's
body died a long time ago now, and he has been
walking in the stars and shining down upon you
each day and night since he left his body.

At night and in the day when you lie down to
sleep, Teala, the light fairy, comes and carries
you and Torah up to Daddy, to walk and laugh
and play. Yahoo! And you know, Evania, Daddy
can laugh and play and cuddle you in his light
body, in your dreams and wishes, and yet he
cannot come back in his body to be with you now.

When Daddy had his crash, his body died. His
spirit and his light went to heaven. As you look
outside at night you can see him shining love and
light down on you. Daddy talks to you and loves
you very much and one day you will truly be
together again.

If any time you feel sad and want to see Daddy,
close your eyes, take some deep breaths and ask

Teala to carry you in her arms to see Daddy.
Teala is a friend of Daddy, Mummy, Torah,
Grandma Alice, Mike, Bay, Luke, Byron, Caleb
and everyone. You can especially help your
mother when she feels sad, or you feel sad, by
remembering Teala, remembering her love.
Look at the stars and know you and Daddy walk
together in your dreams and sleep, dancing and
happy to be together.

God bless you, Evania my love, and fairy blessings to you all.

Mike and Sue

I still cannot read this beautiful letter without tears and
I admit to some envy of the children who are still 'pure'
enough to be able to truly experience Teala and David in
their dreams in this way. Perhaps I also will rediscover
that truth and be able to go with Teala to laugh and dance
with David.

Now at night when Ketorah wakes crying for Daddy I
encourage her to ask Teala the light fairy to take her to
Daddy as she sleeps. A few nights ago we talked in this
way. A little while later I readjusted Ketorah's bedclothes
and she was disturbed as she slept. She cried a gentle,
distant-sounding, 'Daddy!' It was as though she was wi⁺'
him in her dreaming and my 'interference' drew her away
from him. I was torn apart by her cry and as I stood beside
her bed I asked Teala to return Ketorah to her Daddy as
she slept.

Ketorah is now two years and four months old. I suspect
that some of the skills I have learned while working with
Evania will be increasingly appropriate to use with Ketorah
as she becomes more aware of the loss of her physical Daddy.

It is interesting that as Evania and I are letting go more and more of the physical David, Ketorah is becoming more and more aware of the loss of her physical Daddy. And so yet another new chapter of the process begins!

# 11  Stay together

What I am about to write now may not be relevant to you.
You may not be able to identify at all with what I say. You
may feel so secure in your parenting that you may even be
shocked that I, or anyone else, would feel this way. If this
is so for you, then you are greatly blessed. For those few
(perhaps?) who do identify with what I am about to say, I
hope that it will provide some comfort and encouragement.

These thoughts were triggered by a letter I wrote to a
friend whose wife died shortly after David. He was left
with two little girls, one of whom was only a few months
old.

In such situations there may be pressure from within
oneself, or from others, to place the little baby in the care
of someone else, at least for a time. In my situation I
sensed that pressure from within, rather than from others.
People seem to expect that a mother is naturally more able
to cope on her own with children than is a father.

When David was alive I considered him to be the primary parent in many ways. He was forever patient with
the children and, as I saw it, had much more to offer them
than did I. He was a wonderful parent and loved children
in general. I, in contrast, until recently had not felt
comfortable with children and certainly did not regard
myself as a good parent. It would not have been difficult
for me to convince myself that someone else could care for
the children more satisfactorily than I.

As much as I rebelled against it at times, I knew without

a doubt that I had been given this responsibility, by God, the Universe, the Cosmos, the Creator, and that it had not occurred by chance. Rather, I was the one, no matter what I thought, who was to give these little ones what they needed. No one, in fact, could do the job better, otherwise I would not have been chosen. Had I opted out of that responsibility the children would have suffered a second loss, the loss of their mother as well as their father.

Who else could truly be there, for Ketorah in particular, when she woke at night in her grief. Who else could tell her of her relationship with her Daddy, who else be so deeply with her in her loss? In my inadequacy, in my helplessness, I was still the one.

And not only was it important for the children, it was a gift for me as well, perhaps the most beautiful gift I will ever receive. As each day passes, I appreciate still more the wonder of what our tragic experience has produced in terms of the relationships the children and I have. We have all struggled in the dark, together. I have struggled in my parenting, together we have struggled with our grief. We have developed a deep respect for and trust of each other, as well as a more profound love.

So if you are experiencing pressure from yourself or others to relinquish your children into the care of someone else, even for a time, consider very carefully before doing so. Explore all possible and apparently impossible avenues of practical and emotional support which might enable you to get through it together.

We are blessed with wonderfully caring and supportive family doctors, as well as staff at the Katoomba Hospital who, during a period of utter desperation for me, made it possible for us all to have some 'time out' there. The children were admitted to the children's ward where they had a wonderful time, relishing the extra attention and stimulation. I was accommodated comfortably next to the ward and could be as involved with the children as I wanted to be. We were still together **and** I was able to have some time and space to myself, relieved of the responsibility of full-time care of the children. I could be on my own and at the same time there was always someone to talk to if I wanted. During sleepless nights I could get up and have a 'cuppa' with the night sister or a chat with the supervisor.

It was an unutterably valuable opportunity for which I am extremely grateful. I consider that such preventative medicine is a much under-utilised aspect of hospital care and I give credit to our hospital here for being open to it.

One of the other ways of being supported so that you are able to stay together is to make use of the local day care centre. Do not hesitate to seek help from your family doctor or other professionals in recommending your case to be urgently considered. It usually involves a brief letter from the doctor and most such centres have the ability to attend positively to such needs.

Family day care is another option. In this programme children are cared for in the home of another parent, usually a mother who is at home caring for her own children. Both day care centres and family day care programmes are subsidised and the fee is based on your income.

A further possibility is an au pair or a nanny, live-in or on a daily basis. Now before you throw up your hands in horror, amusement, or assume that nannies are only for the wealthy, do take time to consider this option. It need not be a financial impossibility. A live-in au pair might be a part-time student, appreciating accommodation in return for sharing the care of the children, or similarly, someone who is unemployed who might receive full board in return for a specific number of hours a week with the children.

Six months after David died we had, for two or three months, temporary live-in nannies, thanks to the care and initiative of my sister-in-law who flew up from Adelaide when I was feeling desperate. Within hours of her arrival she had organised a nanny to arrive the following day.

It was wonderful to have someone taking over the daily responsibility of the children, to know that there was someone there at night if I needed help with them. They woke frequently during the night in those times. It also enabled me to go out at night without having to plan and organise ahead, something which I seemed quite incapable of doing for at least a year after David died.

Agencies are the quickest and easiest way of finding a nanny. We have drawn on the resources of several such agencies and they are to be highly recommended.

It is helpful to have a list of people on whom you can call. Have the list of names and phone numbers near the phone so that in a moment of crisis you do not have to try and think of someone.

One night when I was desperate with the children, I phoned our very dear friend, Tony. 'Can you come round?' I cried into the mouthpiece. 'Straight away' was his unquestioning response. No explanations were required and he was there in ten minutes, helping me put the children to bed and giving me the opportunity to talk out some of my grief as well. Such are true friends.

There may be people you know who work night-shifts whom you could phone at work to have a chat if you need to. I once phoned David's sister in England at three in the morning. I was desperate to talk to someone and I knew she would still be awake as it was evening there. I do not recommend such drastic measures if you can find someone on a local call!

While researching the appendix to this book, I have discovered that there are organisations offering twenty-four-hour telephone support, specifically for those experiencing grief. (You will find details of these in the appendix.)

In the early days after David died, there were occasions when, for various reasons, I could find no one to help during a crisis period. Weekends were the most difficult times for me and of course community agencies were closed and friends were often out or away, engaged in their own family activities. Following our time in the hospital, a support system was set up to cover such times.

In situations such as yours and ours it is difficult to know what you need, much less how to get it. With these thoughts, I urge you to seek out someone, family doctor, social worker, grief counsellor, anyone who can help you set up such a support system.

There is a way for you all to stay together without going crazy. It may not seem obvious to you at the moment. I hope my suggestions will give you encouragement to explore possibilities.

If after exploring all avenues you still need to place your little one in the care of someone else, then do it without guilt if you can. Know that you have looked at alternatives and that at the moment there is no other way. Make certain that your child does not carry guilt about the separation. Explain why it must be so, no matter how young and uncomprehending you think he or she is.

Make use of the separation to nourish yourself and to be with your process, preferably seeking help with that. Spend as much time as is possible with your child, without putting pressure on yourself to do so. If you are being truthful with yourself in the separation, and with your child, you will all be blessed.

Continue to support your little ones in their process. Relieved of the full-time responsibility you may well find, as I did, that you are more able to be truly 'there' for them, more able to respond to their needs in relation to their grief.

# 12 Inner work: the way through

The intention of this book is not to discuss my own inner journey, the grief process, except as it relates to the children. It is important, however, to say what is perhaps obvious, that the children's process and my work with them cannot be isolated from my own process. Behind what I have written about the children is the story of much hard work as I travelled my own journey. Let there be no risk of you assuming that I was some kind of therapist with knowledge, expertise and skills at my finger-tips, which I was then able to use easily in relation to the children. What I have done and continue to do comes very much out of my own process.

And you, as parent in this situation, cannot expect to be able to support your precious little charges in their grief if you are not working with your own process. The progress of your child at this stage will be directly related to your own work. If you are committed to your own inner journey, then your little one will experience the process positively. If, on the other hand, you are resisting your own process, it is more than likely that your child will be 'stuck' as well.

For those of you who are committed to your own journey, be assured that, on the very basis of that fact, you will be able to appropriately support your child.

If you have not been committed to your process so far, or if what I have just said sounds like some sort of esoteric nonsense, then I urge you to take an hour or so to be quietly on your own, asking yourself what this means and how it relates to you. If you do this with a genuine desire to see what is going on for you, then you will find the answer, even if that answer is to seek someone who can help you look at this issue.

What did I do in relation to my own journey? That is perhaps another book! I will, however, briefly relate some of the ways in which I worked with my process.

The first and most important thing is to **allow** the process to occur. And that does not mean only for the first few weeks or months. It means the whole process, however long it takes. It most certainly will not be completed in six months. In fact, in my experience and those of others I know, the process often becomes even more difficult during the six- to twelve-months period. I suspect that part of the reason this is so is that others around us, and ourselves as well, expect that we should be feeling 'better' by then, 'getting on with life'. We are less inclined to feel 'okay' about the tears, the lack of energy, depression, anger, and still the incredible disbelief.

It is also true that the shock and numbness wears off and as the days, weeks and months pass, the reality of that most unbelievable fact becomes more and more apparent. The sense of loss and emptiness seems to be intensified still further.

Six months after David died, I wrote in my journal:

> David, David, David...
> When will I ever believe, much less accept that you, as I knew you in this life, have gone forever, died...
> When will I ever stop remembering the sixth of

April with utter disbelief and shock? The disbelief is more intense (as are all my feelings) as
each day passes.
O David, **when** will I believe,
**when** will I accept,
**when** will I stop crying...

If only I could get some relief from the pain, even
for a few days...or hours...
It's there...THERE...here, right on the surface.
When I'm not crying, I feel like crying.
No relief, no bloody relief.
I can't believe what happened to you.
I can't believe what's happening to me...the
pain...the intensity...

The children, **our** children...
Evania speaks of you **so** often now, several times
a day.
Is it hitting her as it is me?
'Daddy come home soon?'
'Daddy come see me?'
And her chanting in the car the other day:
'Daddy died, Daddy died,
Daddy died, died, died.
Daddy, Daddy died.'

The other day I wore your dustcoat when I was
working. When Evania came home, she ran over
to it, 'Daddy come see me?'
She talks to herself about you, and to her dolls
and teddies, 'Daddy, my Daddy'.

I can't believe this incredible hole I'm in, we're
in.

I **know** that this hole is creative.

I'm aware that I'm more in touch with myself, more centred than possibly ever before. I have such strong feelings about whether or not something is right for me, a clarity I've never experienced.

And yet I want to get out of this hole. I want desperately to have relief from the pain.

The only way out of it is THROUGH it, I know that.

AND I want OUT.

\*      \*      \*

In practical terms, one of the tools I used to express my grief, to be with the grief in a conscious sense, was drawing. Each evening in the early weeks, and several times a week later on I gave myself an hour to do a drawing. They were abstract drawings which expressed my confidence and my fears, the pain and the beauty, my sense of weakness and the strengths, my despair and my hope.

Before beginning a drawing, I sat quietly for a few minutes, becoming still and more centred. When beginning each drawing I had no idea what the final result would be. It was rather like a meditation. Almost always by the time I completed the drawing I felt more grounded, centred and at peace. I do not understand how it happens. I do know that in the process of doing the drawing something moved in my inner process. Very rarely was I conscious of what that was. I only knew that something had moved. The actual doing of the drawing was more important than the completed drawing.

As a way of honouring the drawing as part of my process, I used good quality materials—paper and soft pastels. The completed drawing was placed in a prominent position where I could refer to it during the following day. The more powerful drawings found permanent wall-space and the less meaningful ones were replaced each day by the succeeding drawing.

Writing has always been a helpful tool for me. After David died, I wrote...and wrote...long letters to friends about my experience, entries in my ever-handy journal, letters to David. I found it very helpful to get on to paper what was happening and in the writing of it I often achieved greater clarity and almost always received comfort from being able to express myself in this way. I hasten to clarify the fact that the drawings and writing did not often make me 'feel better'. Often they led me into more grief. My point is that these tools helped me to stay with the process, and honour it.

Dialogue was a particularly powerful tool at times in those early months, when I would tell David what was happening for me and allow him to respond to that. One of those dialogues went something like this:

Heather:    O David, these last ten days or so have been **so** difficult, much more difficult than I had expected in view of how strong I'd felt in the first week. However, today there has been a breakthrough as a result of spending some time with E.C. One of the things that came out of that time is that I'm impatient!

David:      Typical!

Heather:    Yes, I know, I'm expecting...

David:      Expectations again, eh?

| | |
|---|---|
| Heather: | Yes!  I know!  Anyway I'm expecting it all to be done quickly, and it is only three weeks today since you left us ...<br>LEFT US!<br>YOU LEFT US!<br>**YOU LEFT US!**<br>HOW COULD YOU HAVE DONE IT??<br>**HOW COULD YOU?**<br>And now I can feel myself blocking my feelings again. |
| David: | Mm, and having a glass of wine to push it all down. |
| Heather: | Yes, and **you're** not the one having to deal with all this, so who are you to talk!  I'm going to have a glass of wine as my treat to myself at the end of the day, and I'm going to do it because **I** want to. |
| David: | That's okay, as long as you're aware of what you are doing, that you are pushing down the grief. |
| Heather: | Yes, yes ...<br>Anyway, getting back to my time with E.C.  It was so reassuring to be reminded that your essence, your spirit is available to me if I am open to you.  And our relationship can become even stronger.  Even more reassuring is the knowledge that through my openness to your spirit, the girls will also know you.<br>I suppose the most difficult thing has been the fact that my dearest—**our** very dearest little ones—will grow up without a father, and people have been telling me that even Evania |

won't remember you.

O David, please beat my brains out if necessary in order for me to remember all of that and to open myself to your spirit.

How wonderful to think that our spirits can be closer than ever, and that the children will know you in an even deeper way also.

David:     I keep telling you that everything is perfect!

Heather:   Yes, I know, you're always right!

David:     I know!

Heather:   Mm, I suppose I've no hope of ever catching you out now!

David:     Nup!

Heather:   Gee, it's nice talking to you like this. One of the things I've missed so much is telling you about the daily events. You were always carrying on about me suddenly remembering things I'd forgotten to tell you about the day. You wanted to know it all. I've been finding myself thinking that I must remember to tell David such and such. Or 'Won't David be interested to hear **that**!' And this way I can still do it.

David:     No...! And it's taken you all this time to discover it!

Heather:   Well, in your mother's words, 'We can't all be perfect!' How could you! Gee I love you! How could you leave us? We had such a wonderful relationship...

such exquisite children...

everything was going so well...

David:     And still is.

Heather:    Be quiet! I know, it's all perfect'. But you're not here and it feels anything but perfect!

David:    And it is.

Heather:    I repeat, BE QUIET.

I've realised that I must arrange to have some time without the children, speaking of whom, one is awake, so I must go...

Though rather a light-hearted affair, it was amazing how helpful that little bit of dialogue was. Afterwards I had more energy, perhaps because I felt more in touch with David and more hopeful about our continuing relationship.

A few days later I continued:

Heather:    O David, David, how hard it has been, and is. I keep expecting it to get easier and I suspect that what is really happening is that I'm allowing myself to get more in touch with the reality, more in touch with my grief, the sense of deep loss, deep loss and emptiness. This evening I even thought that if I could be sure that it would be as clean as your accident, I'd set one up for Evania, Ketorah and myself.

I expected it to be difficult and I didn't know what that would mean. It's been more difficult than I could ever have anticipated. I simply cannot believe that in an instant your physical presence has gone from us forever—with absolutely no warning. If you had been going away to meditate on top of a mountain in India, even if forever, there would have been at least a brief time of preparation as you bought your ticket, or whatever.

David: And if you'd needed warning or preparation, there would have been the time. In fact there was, as you've been telling people and as you can see in retrospect. You were prepared well. All was and is PERFECT.

Heather: Yes, and I guess I know that. Sometimes I even think what a miracle it was that you died the way you did, for I cannot think of a more perfect way, instant, without warning, 'clean'. I guess neither of us needed warning and preparation. We must have both been ready or else it would have been different.
AND it's still bloody difficult!

David: Yes, and no matter how many good things you see about it all, there **are** still immense difficulties, though certainly not insurmountable.

Heather: O David, how I miss you! Will I ever come out of this deep, deep sense of loss. There is such an immense emptiness which NO ONE, NO THING, NO ACTIVITY will **ever** fill. There was **so** much in our relationship.
I am thankful for that.
There are very few couples who would have a relationship with anything like the quality of ours. What an honour, a privilege, a great, great gift. And yet the very preciousness of it is what makes the loss so great.

\*　　\*　　\*

As well as entering into dialogue with a person it can also be helpful to have dialogue with a part of yourself, perhaps your aching back, or with a feeling, for example your grief or anger. To do this with a character from a dream is also often very productive.

Though not very skilled in the area of dreams, I did diligently record my dreams and work with them as best I could. Knowing from the work of Carl Jung that each character in the dream represents an aspect of myself enabled me to get more in touch with those parts of myself.

It is important that you have time for yourself. The evenings when the children were asleep were very precious to me. Apart from the sounds of the bush (and believe me, that can be considerable on a still evening!), there was total silence and that in itself was nourishing. The evenings were my 'working' times, the times for drawing and writing.

As well as work times, it is essential that you have times to nourish yourself in 'be-nice-to-yourself' ways. That is sometimes, or rather often, not as easy as it sounds. I found it difficult to even know what I could do to nourish and nurture myself, apart from working hard on the inner 'stuff'. Over a period of a week or so I made a list of such things: a hot bath with lovely oils in it, or a forest walk. One of my favourite treats at that time was to have half an hour or so to sit in a coffee shop and have coffee and cake. I think the attraction of this was that I was able to be out in the world without directly relating to people.

A massage, a trip to the hairdresser, a facial, were all on my list. This kind of physical contact was healing, especially during a period when I felt that I did not want touch in the form of hugs and other physical expressions of affection, except by my children. The children and I have always had heaps of wonderfully nourishing physical contact.

A few weeks after David died I bought some clay, and sculpturing was a source of great nourishment.

It seems to me a natural law that unless you are being nourished yourself, you cannot expect to be able to provide rich nourishment for your children. The teapot will not give endless cups of tea without more being put into it. You cannot give out endlessly without nourishing yourself well. It is also important for the children to see that you do nice things for yourself so that they can learn to do the same for themselves.

For the first six months after David died, I had very little practical support. I stumbled along day by day, doing all the humdrum things as best I could, caring for two very young children, breast-feeding Ketorah. There were all the usual chores, washing, cooking, keeping the house in some sort of order, shopping, bringing in wood for the huge and ever-hungry slow combustion stove which also provides our hot water and heating. I was also trying to complete the second stage of our building project as we lived in a very small completed part of the house. I spent evenings putting up plaster wall-board and plastering. I continued to be involved in the landscaping business, helping Jim with quotes, ordering materials and making up a portfolio of our work. There were anxieties about finance. I was fortunate to have a small income and my family is well-off financially. Although there were grumblings about my requests for financial assistance, I knew that I could get help from my family in this way. For others in such a situation there may be more complicated financial difficulties.

It would have been easy to immerse myself in the practical things of life. I knew, however, that it was crucial that I make time, no matter how difficult that was (and you could not, I assure you, underestimate those difficulties!), to be with my grief in a direct way and to do some nice things for myself. I was chronically tired, with low levels of energy at the best of times. I found that I did feel clearer and had a little more energy when I made the effort to set aside these all-important times for myself.

In order to do this I responded to friends' offers of help by asking them to have the children for a couple of hours. I did not find it at all easy to request help from friends. To ask someone for something for myself was a new and uncomfortable experience. The voice of conditioning prattled on in my head, 'Who are you to ask people to look after your children while you go out for coffee or have a massage? What right have you to expect that? Who do you think you are?' The more I ignored the voice, the fainter it became and the easier it was to take up the offers of help from friends.

If you also have difficulties about asking for help from friends, family, neighbours, I hope that by hearing about my struggle in relation to this, you will be encouraged to try reaching out in this way, no matter how uncomfortable it feels at first.

\* \* \*

For the first six months after David died, I felt all right about the process. It was painful. It was hard work. And I felt that it was moving well. At about the six-months point I became aware that I needed some very skilled help. I knew that the grief had moved me into unresolved areas of my life. I did not know what those areas were. I knew only that there was something there which must be attended to.

To this end I contacted our very dear friend in Western Australia, Mike Sowerby. We arranged to meet half-way, in Adelaide, for some intensive therapy. At an isolated shack on the coast, we spent five days together, working round the clock. We had a second such intensive work-period two months later, in the meantime continuing the work through phone calls, letters and cassettes. Mike and I worked together for some months after this second time together in Adelaide, and without this opportunity I suspect that I would not be here today. There were indeed many unresolved issues which had been laid bare by the grieving process and which needed attention.

It was clear that as I worked my way through these issues, I was more able to respond appropriately to the needs of the children in their grief. More than that, I noticed that as I removed each layer of my inner mess, it seemed to clear the way for Evania to express more of her grief. The clearest example of this is what I believe was a direct relationship between my work with Mike in Adelaide the second time and the clearer expression of Evania's grief almost immediately following that. It was as though she knew at some level that I would now be able to cope with her grief more satisfactorily and so she was free to express it.

One of the significant experiences which led to a profound change in the depth of my relationships with the children came at about the time of the first anniversary of David's death.

After my time with Mike in February, ten months after

David's death, I began to search for something I could do for someone else. I continued to be very much focused on myself and the children, there were still the symptoms of earlier months, lethargy, disbelief, tears. I certainly did not **feel** like going out to help someone else. With Mike's urging I did so.

On a notice-board in the local shopping centre, I found an advertisement for volunteers at the nearby psychiatric hospital. Volunteers were sought to help in a wide variety of programmes so I arranged to see the appropriate members of the staff there. We went through the seventeen programmes available. It was not until we came to the last programme on the list that I found the one that was right for me.

Each Friday I spent a couple of hours with the dementia patients, participating in a sing-song for them. It was perfect. I enjoyed it immensely and found myself being nourished by these patients. I spent a few minutes with each of four or five of them during each half-hour session and while I sang all the old songs with great gusto, I maintained eye contact with whichever patient I was beside, holding her hand or placing my hand on his shoulder.

These dear people nourished me through that eye contact with what I can only describe as pure love. They were unable to converse and often sat there without the slightest response, or so it seemed. But the love in their eyes during that prolonged eye contact was anything but unresponsive!

What an incredibly healing experience it was.

Several weeks after this began I became aware that I was having the same contact with Evania and Ketorah. It was as though our souls met at some deep level where there is no time and space, no age in terms of years of life on this earth. Those dear dementia patients had given me a priceless gift which I was then able to recognise in my relationships with the children.

It seems that I was able to become aware of that kind of connection with someone when the 'trappings' of intellect, conversation, appearance, personality were not so evident. I was able to see past what in other social situations would probably have engaged my interest and attention, to what I believed to have been the essence, the true being of these dear people.

And then, even more precious was the discovery of that kind of relating with my own precious little ones.

# 13   Issues for mothers...
## for fathers...

The issues I have discussed so far are, I trust, equally
relevant to men and women. I would now like to address
some issues which are more specific to women, or to men.

It is possible for young children in our society to have
very little or no contact with men. Women have until
recently been given and have accepted full responsibility
for child care in our society. As a result of their ability to
carry and give birth to children, the expectation generally
has been that women have a natural ability to care for
children and by implication men lack this. We are slowly
discovering and accepting that this is not necessarily so.
I have met a number of men who are not only sharing the
parenting of their children, but whose work outside the
home is in the area of child care. In spite of these changes,
women still carry the major responsibility for child care,
not only in the home but in day care centres, pre-schools,
as baby-sitters, or nursing sisters.

Women need to be aware of the importance of male
figures in the lives of their children. Some will have caring
men in their families and/or circles of friends to discuss
the importance of male involvement in the life of the
family. Raising it directly will help clarify the issue for
everyone.

Those who lack such male figures in their family life will
need to be open to opportunities which present themselves

in day-to-day life. Chatting over the fence to the retired neighbour, watching the men who work around the house or in the streets nearby, greeting a shop assistant—all this can help. Children will, as I have indicated earlier, find ways of having their needs met if adults are open to this. My children were drawn to male figures and we spent hours watching men dig holes in the footpath to repair a cable, cut grass at the park, unload newspapers at the news-stand. Evania was especially good at seeking out caring male figures and we have some wonderful men-friends as a result of her initial contact. Of course there is need for caution as we hear almost daily of children being abused by men. That such incidents occur is undeniable. It is also true that there are wonderful caring men out there and we must be careful not to exclude, through fear, the possibility of male involvement in the lives of our children.

The father who has suffered the loss of his partner, and now has full responsibility for the care of his children, will almost certainly experience pressure to relinquish the children into the care of others. This may or may not come from family and close friends. It will certainly come in direct and indirect ways from many in our society. I would like to encourage you, the bereaved father who reads this book, to spend some time (if you have not already done so) clarifying the matter of what you want most in relation to the care of your children. Specifically, do you want to continue in the tradition of women caring for the children, or do you want to exercise your own right to be the primary carer? If you decide in favour of the latter, you must be very clear in your own mind so that you can, in turn, be clear with others about what you want.

Today I was speaking to a solo father who has cared for his now school-age daughter since she was a baby. He commented that there is pressure on the male solo parent to be seen to be producing the goods. Solo fathers attract stricter and more critical condemnation than do mothers in the same situation. He added that this can result in the risk of paranoia. This same father emphasised the privilege of having had the opportunity to be so closely involved in the life of his daughter and now speaks with authority six years after making the decision to care for his child.

As a father considering the available options you are particularly vulnerable in the early weeks and months following the loss of your partner, when it would be so easy to hand over the responsibility to women eager, available and sympathetic, as well as experienced in the care of children. It is most important in this situation for you to find someone who is able to support you in considering the options open to you. This person may be a friend who is able to help you look more clearly at the options and who has some objectivity. Or it may be a professional. Whoever it is, you must feel confident in their willingness to assist you in doing what you want to do. You do not need someone who is merely pandering to you and who hopes to eventually convince you of the impossibility of your aims. Continue searching until you find the right person.

In the short term try to get some extended leave from work so that you have the opportunity to test your decision and explore the support of the community, family and friends. Wherever possible, major and irreversible decisions should not be made by anyone who is in a state of grief.

It is accepted that mothers caring for young children at

home can become socially isolated and long for the stimulation of adult conversation.  A father who has accepted
the expectation that he will always be the breadwinner
and his wife the homemaker, and who suddenly finds
himself looking at the home and children as his sole
responsibility, has adjustments to make.  With the help of
friends or professionals, he must take at least as much care
as the solo mother to see that he has time for himself and
some social outlets.

Ideally, it should be possible for the father to remain at
work if he so chooses, perhaps reducing the work-load to
part-time.  So far men lack the lobby groups to raise in our
society, and among employer groups and politicians, the
awareness of these issues.  It should be possible to have
part-time work, or take the computer home and work from
there, or job-share.  In general terms our society is even
less supportive of a father's need to do this than of a
woman's need.

There are some further practical issues which relate
only to fathers.  One of these is what to do when your
young daughter needs to use a public toilet.  The same
problem does not arise when a young son is out with his
mother and needs to go to the toilet.  In many shopping
centres there are mothers' rooms, places where nappies
can be changed, bottoms washed and babies fed, but these
are usually part of the complex containing the women's
toilets.  They are unavailable to fathers who are caring for
their babies.  There are a surprising number of men who
are caring for young babies without the help of the mother
and society has certainly not yet caught up with even the
most basic needs of these courageous fathers.

For those of you facing the basic practical issues mentioned above, my suggestion is that you do what other fathers I know have done—simply feel your way through the issues, remaining clear in your purpose and not allowing yourselves to be intimidated by others. You have every right to do what you are doing and you are to be congratulated.

# 14 The professional care-giver

So far this book has been addressed to those most inti-
mately involved following the death of a parent of young
children—the remaining parent or partner and to some
extent close friends. This book would not be complete,
though, without reference to the professional who may
become involved with the grieving family, in particular the
children of the dead parent. In our own situation this has
included doctors, nursing staff in the children's ward of
the local hospital, a social worker, grief counsellor and day
care centre staff. Others who could be expected to become
involved with such a family would be pre-school staff and
school teachers, priests, ministers and pastors. These and
numerous other health care workers are those to whom I
address this chapter.

Much of what I have already written will of course be
helpful to you as a professional and I will include some of
those points again here as a summary.

Perhaps the clearest understanding to come out of my
contact with, and support of, people in grief is that the
experience of each person is very different. It is very easy
for professionals who have undertaken some study of the
subject, and who have experience of grief in others as well
as themselves, to have expectations about how it should
be for people who are grieving. The more I see of people
in such circumstances, the more I realise how different it
is for each person.

Grief is a **normal** part of life which no one can avoid.

The grieving process will be different for each person according to their conditioning in relation to death and loss, the experiences they have had in other situations of pain and difficulty and the inner resources they can draw on.

Reading on the subject and experience with those in grief reveal that some patterns do emerge, that denial, anger, disbelief, bargaining, acceptance are common to most people who are grieving. What I want to say here is that care needs to be given to avoid focusing on the common aspects of the process at the expense of the differences. I have discovered that I need to be more alert than ever in order to leave aside my expectations, understanding and experiences when I am with people in grief, so that I can be truly present to each of them in **their** individual process.

This is particularly so with very young children who, I believe, can teach **us** rather than we them about death and the processes involved in relation to it. They are less conditioned by our society and more in touch with the realities of death.

As a member of a society in which there are so many unresolved issues about death, I am aware that there are still areas in my own life which remain unresolved and which will be triggered by my contact with others in grief. I aim to be constantly alert to anything needing attention in relation to this.

I am particularly alert to any discomfort I feel when with someone in grief. Perhaps it is something he or she has said, or some behaviour exhibited. I may want to 'correct', modify, interrupt or contradict something said, some part of an experience. Such discomfort is a signal that there is in myself some unresolved area about the issues of death and loss. It is certainly not a matter of questioning the validity of what she is saying, what he is experiencing. It is my own discomfort, nothing to do with the other person, and in being aware of this discomfort I am less likely to project it on to those I am trying to support.

Often the awareness alone is enough to begin resolving the issue. If not, I have various strategies including seeking outside support from perhaps a supervisor, counsellor or therapist to further the process. I do this for my own sake, and to increase the effectiveness of my work with others.

One of the indicators I watch for are words which surface such as 'bizarre'. Often what we think of as bizarre, especially in relation to death, is really very healthy. A professional person in a senior position came to see me recently about someone with whom she was working. One of the things which concerned her was the 'bizarre' behaviour of her client. After only brief discussion it was clear that these concerns were unwarranted and we spent the rest of the time looking at why she had difficulty accepting healthy aspects of the grieving process. As a result of this professional's unresolved issues it was impossible for her at that time to support her client in a necessary part of the grieving process. The effectiveness of the staff for whom she was responsible, and her supervision of them and their casework, were also at risk of being limited.

What I learn from others in grief is immeasurable when I lay aside, at least temporarily, the knowledge, theories and expectations I have gathered, and open myself to the experience of those who are there in the midst of it. Attitudes to death in our society have been and for the most part continue to be unhealthy and unrealistic and there is still much to be learnt by those of us who work in the area.

Another signal in myself of unresolved issues about death, loss of any kind and the accompanying grief, is any feeling experienced which is intense enough to affect my functioning in the situation. Common examples are sadness, the intensity of which can result in uncontrolled weeping, or anger leading to a lack of clarity. God forbid that I be interpreted as saying that I must always be in control of my emotions, that I should be the passive, unmoved, unfeeling professional, such that we were taught to be in the 1960s! Nothing is further from my intention. It is possible, however, to be mistaken in relation to the **intensity** of such feelings. There would indeed be need for concern if I did not have feelings of sadness, for example, when with someone in grief. It is healthy and appropriate. If the sadness reaches a point of being overwhelming, it is more than certainly related to some unresolved grief of my own. I need to acknowledge that, to myself certainly, and probably to the person I am with and aiming to support. What I do in a situation where I am no longer functioning can be creative rather than harmful to myself and the client if I am honest about it. Then of course it is important afterwards to deal with the issue which has arisen, triggered by the grief of the other person.

Though not in a professional role at the time, I experienced something like this a few weeks ago. A group I was in received news of the death of the husband of a member. I had a reasonably close relationship with the woman and had met her husband. I felt great sadness for my friend and wept for her. The intensity of my sadness soon became overwhelming: I could no longer function in the group and had to remove myself temporarily. I recognised almost immediately that my friend's situation had been a trigger for expression of more of my own grief in relation to David's death. I allowed myself to be in that emotional space for as long as I needed; then I returned to the group. I had cleared a little more of my own grief and was now able to support my friend.

Such incidents can trigger grief from times long gone and for losses almost forgotten. If we are alert to what is happening, give attention to our feelings and the possible source of them, we will be available to healing for ourselves. As a result we will be more available to others who are in need of our support.

During my own professional training in one of the helping professions there was a complete failure to acknowledge the reality of unresolved areas in our lives and of their significance in our work with others. I regard attention to the resolution of these areas as they arise as a part, in fact the most important part, of my on-going professional development.

In my own experience of the grieving parent of young grieving children, the projections of professionals was one of the most frustrating and least helpful aspects of the process. It was a painful experience being 'on the other end' of the helping professions. It confirmed my already existing belief that I have an enormous responsibility not to add extra burdens to those I aim to help by loading them up with my own unresolved issues. To avoid this, as far as is possible, requires constant attention to what is happening for me, as well as the obvious responsibility of being aware of what is happening for the other person, of his or her needs.

## Your presence with the grieving child

Professionals working in the home, office or clinic will be in one-to-one contact with the grieving child. The other environment most common to professionals having contact with these children is the day-care centre, pre-school and school. Both these aspects give opportunities for helping the child.

It is very important that children in grief have contact with those who are not immediately involved with the death, that there are more 'normal' things going on in their lives alongside the grief process. Certainly in the very early few days it is important for the family to be together in their grief. (I shudder when I hear that a child has been removed to stay with a relative for a few days immediately after the death.)

The most helpful aspect of what professionals have to offer is to be totally there with the child. That is a very precious gift in itself at any time and especially at a time of loss when grieving adults are in such pain that they cannot be totally present to anyone else. This is even more so in relation to very young children who, as we have seen earlier, are not expected to grieve.

If the professional provides space for the child it is more than likely that the child will provide clues to what he or she needs in the contact time.

A walk was one of the activities my girls most loved when someone had time for them. That assumes that the child feels comfortable in being separated from the parent, and I am aware of the children for whom separation is painful. A walk emphasises that the person accompanying the child has set aside this time solely for her or for him. The activity allows more freedom of thought and emotions for a young child than does sitting still. During the walk there is opportunity to express some of the frustration by perhaps kicking the fallen autumn leaves about, running in the park or experiencing the wind while being pushed high on a swing. There may be comfort for the little one in hugging a tree, throwing stones into a creek or drawing with a stick on the ground. It may be that sitting in a gutter and having a lovely warm cuddle is what the child needs.

If you feel that the behaviour while you are on your walk indicates some feeling specifically related to the child's loss, it is helpful to comment on that. 'Are you feeling angry about Daddy not being here?' 'Perhaps you are feeling sad about Daddy.' If your perception is inaccurate, it will be rejected without any harm having being caused. If you are right, it will comfort the little one to know that you understand some of what is happening in his inner world. It will also give him the opportunity to respond further to your comment, open up a little more to his process, express some more of his grief.

It may be appropriate on a windy day to allow a special leaf as a gift or message to be taken by the wind to the parent who has died. Perhaps you could help the young child to gather some things on the walk which can be made into a little shrine or altar or remembering place in some little corner of the park or family garden. If there is a creek nearby or fast running water in the gutters, a flower or leaf or stick can be sent down the stream, a symbol of the connection which continues to exist between the child and the dead parent, the sending of love and a sharing of the feelings of the little one with the spirit or essence of that parent.

Incidentally, all these little rituals can be just as meaningful and helpful to adults in grief.

For professionals confined to the office, clinic or the home of the child, there are, as with the walk, a variety of things that can help.

One of the activities I have found most helpful is drawing. As long as the child is old enough to be able to hold a crayon it is likely that drawing will be of interest. I suggest that you have a supply of suitable paper and some crayons in your office and that if you are going to the home of the child, you take them with you. Having your own supply will serve two purposes, one is that it will be something special for the child and the other is that members of the family will not have to find the materials.

Drawing is an excellent activity for expression of feelings, for adults as well as children. For children it is even more helpful because their language skills may be limited or almost non-existent. The value of such expression, no matter how scribbly and seemingly without form and meaning, should not be under-estimated.

Comment on the drawing and ask questions about it, especially if you notice something which gives you a clue to what is going on for the child. Perhaps your clue will be in the energy put into the drawing, perhaps in the colours used. (Make sure you provide a wide range of colours.) The drawing may give you and the little one an opportunity to further explore the feelings of that time. When the drawing is finished, the child may wish to send it to the parent who has died—to post it, burn it, send it out to sea, down the stream or gutter. Or perhaps it will become a gift for the remaining parent.

As drawing skills develop, it is possible to discover much more about what is in the inner world of the child. I urge anyone involved with children to develop this interest in and understanding of drawings. Gregg Furth has written a book which I have found to be invaluable and details of it are in the list of recommended reading (see p.110). He also conducts workshops from time to time in Australia, the US and other countries.

Where a child's drawings have more form, there are some reasonably simple points to look for. One of the subjects children love to draw is a house. Another is a tree. Both of these can reveal some significant clues about the inner world of the child. The tree, as a symbol of the self, may be particularly small in relation to the size of the paper, indicating the sense of smallness and insignificance the child feels in relation to his or her position in the world. If the tree is dead it reflects how the child feels inside. On the other hand, if the tree is fruitful, lush and healthy, then it reflects the same in the child. I am alerted by a drawing of a dead tree to the urgent need to find more ways of supporting the child in the process, perhaps referring her or him for more specialised help. Again there needs to be discussion with the child about the drawing. It may be that the tree is in fact dormant, that it is winter and the leaves have fallen; spring will bring new growth, in which case it provides a very different perception of the state of the child's process to that of the dead tree.

Some points to notice in the drawing of a house include whether or not the house has a chimney, a symbol of warmth in the home. If there is no door, no way into or out of the house, it can indicate that the child has that same sense of there being no way of anyone coming into his or her world and no way of getting out of it. There is a sense of being quite cut off from the world. Windows that are non-existent, very high or particularly small give us an idea of the relationship to the outside world—it is impossible to see out if the windows are very high: little light is let into the house (representing the inner world of the child) if the windows are particularly small—none at all if there are no windows. Is there a handle on the door, giving entrance to the house? What sort of access is there to the door? Is there a path leading to it? These and many other simple aspects of a drawing can tell us much about what is happening for the child.

When children are old enough to have skills to do such drawings I invariably ask them specifically to do a drawing of a house on one sheet of paper and a tree on another. I have not yet met a child who has not been enthusiastic to meet my request. Often I do the same with adults, especially if it is difficult to form a clear idea of what is happening for them.

The third drawing in this 'diagnostic' series is a person. Again this represents the inner world of the person doing the drawing. If the child is of an age where you would expect drawing skills to include hands and feet, an absence of these can signal a sense of helplessness. Without feet we are, in the physical world, indeed helpless. Is there ground under the figure to support it or is it 'ungrounded', suspended in space?

This series of drawings is a very helpful way of monitoring the process of the child, something which can be done every few weeks. It can also be done in a doctor's surgery while the doctor is involved with another member of the family. Such a drawing serves to give freer space to the presenting patient as well as checking out the child's process. The young one is usually more than happy to do a drawing for the interested doctor-friend, especially if there is a little table and a chair which is specially theirs to use. And of course these drawings will be found useful for children other than those in grief.

I have written elsewhere in this book about sandplay and play therapy. Most professionals having any contact with children will have some toys in the office. These can be used for a sandless sandplay or play therapy. You do not have to have an enormous collection of small toys for the children to do something equivalent to a sandplay on the floor or table. I have used the few bits and pieces most toy collections offer to encourage children to create on the floor a picture similar to that of sandplay.

If you do have frequent opportunities to work with children a more deliberate collection of suitable toys or pieces will be invaluable. A fruit box half-filled with sand will be a very useful piece of equipment and your small collection may even be taken with you when you go on a home visit.

Similarly keep some teddy bears and dolls for use in a play-therapy situation. They can be housed in the office to be taken where appropriate or the dolls and teddies may be found in the home of the child when you visit.

Physical contact is particularly important for the grieving child. Adults should respect the little one's boundaries but contact should be offered as much as possible. Stroking and massage, even if only the feet, will be comforting and healing.

Some suitable music will be an added bonus during any of these non-verbal activities. It has been found that even the unborn foetus relaxes when the music of Vivaldi is played. (The music of Beethoven on the other hand results in the foetus becoming more agitated.) Flute music is also relaxing presumably because of its relative simplicity compared to something like a symphony of Beethoven. As I write this chapter for professionals I am in the last weeks of pregnancy and again this is my experience. When playing the piano, I substitute my favourite Beethoven sonatas for lighter works by composers such as Pachelbel, Scarlatti, Purcell, Handel, Bach and Haydn.

I have found the same reactions are true for young children—and adults. Other music which I have found to be helpful is that of the Incas with their pan pipes, Indian and other Eastern music using bells and more primitive instruments, and some early Christian music such as Gregorian Chant. Book shops selling 'alternative' literature will be able to help you select tapes of the music I have mentioned and of course most record shops will have the works of Vivaldi and music for the flute and pan pipes.

There are some suitable story-books to read to children in grief, including one or two by Elisabeth Kubler-Ross. As well as these books, anything about the life-cycle of a caterpillar is helpful for children dealing with death.

# 15  The grieving child at school

All of what I have said above is of course relevant if teachers are able to spend some time alone with the grieving child. Again, the most important thing to do is to acknowledge the little one's grief. It is important that he or she knows that you know about the sadness. 'I heard about your Daddy dying. You must be feeling very sad. Would you like a cuddle?'

From then on, simply keep an eye on the child who will give you cues to act. It is certainly inappropriate and unproductive to fuss. If you intercept a sad, distant or 'lost' look, you could go and sit beside him or her for a few minutes. Perhaps offer to take a short walk together during one of the breaks. As I have indicated earlier in this book, more difficult behaviours can be a cue to the need for further acknowledgement of the little one's sadness.

It is important to have information about what is happening at home and how the little one seems in relation to that. Two or three minutes with the parent who brings the child to the centre or pre-school will provide that information and will give the parent a sense of your support. Similarly, when the child is collected at the end of the day, you will be able to comment about how the day has been.

It is appropriate to enlist the support of the other children, again without fuss. 'Evania will be feeling sad and lonely at times because her Daddy has died and she misses him very much. We can help her by being gentle

and loving.' I believe that we very much underestimate
the support very young children can give to others. They
are more sincere and spontaneous than many adults are
able to be. A child who does not feel able to support
another child will not become involved, but there need not
be any sense of having rejected the one who is sad. There
will always be some children in the group who can be
beautifully supportive to a child who is hurt and they
should be acknowledged and supported in that role.

Older grieving children can be more complex as they
have already begun to take on their parents' discomfort.

When the subject of death presents itself so directly in
a class of children, there is a wonderful opportunity for the
growth of everyone in the class as well as for providing
support to the child directly affected. Some children will
inevitably ask questions and they need to be answered
directly, simply and clearly. Begin with a little information in response to the question and wait for further
questions and prompting to indicate how you can proceed.

Such times as 'Show and Tell' or daily news-time are
excellent opportunities to include the grieving child's process in the life of the whole class. Contrary to the expectations of many adults the child whose parent has died will
often be quite enthusiastic to share some of that with the
class during news-time. Why would he not want to talk
about the funeral he went to yesterday, just as he would
share with the class any other outing, a new toy or the
visitors who had been part of his day? It may be helpful
to prompt the child: 'I heard that you went to the funeral
yesterday. Would you like to tell us about that?' The child
can respond to the offered opportunity or not without any
harm having been done.

Books which can be read to such classes are listed in the recommended reading. One which can be followed up more directly is the life cycle of the caterpillar which beautifully illustrates the cycle of life, death and new life. If you are able to get hold of some silkworms they will provide an interesting example as their life cycle is followed by the class.

Another symbol of the life-death cycle are the seasons of the year. This is especially relevant if the death has followed an illness. The summer is the symbol of the life of that person before the illness became evident, autumn being the period of 'decline' leading up to death, symbolised by the season of winter. Spring represents the new life which will come to the remaining members of the family as well as to the spirit of the one who has died.

The meaning of this symbolism does not necessarily need to be spelt out to the children. They will have that knowing somewhere in their being and it will come alive as they are presented with the symbols.

Teachers can also be particularly alert to opportunities such as a dead bird in the playground or the death of a class pet. The children can be encouraged to talk about how it might have died, the normality of such an event. They can work out a little ritual surrounding the burial of the little creature. This discussion can extend into information about ways of dealing with a body which has died. Something about what happens in other cultures may be helpfully included.

Such an incident gives an opportunity for the children to talk about how they felt when one of their pets died, or when Grandma or Grandpa died. As well as the normalcy of death being an issue, normal feelings associated with such a loss need also to be addressed. Discussion of this nature not only provides excellent preparation for such events in the future, it also makes possible some resolution of any such losses which have already occurred in the lives of the children.

Of course these opportunities can present themselves at any time but it remains true that teachers will be much more alert to them if there is a child who has just experienced the death of a loved one.

To work creatively with a class in the ways I have suggested will presuppose that teachers are themselves comfortable with the issue. Some parents of children may not be so comfortable and teachers may be confronted with that. If they are approached by such parents, teachers can encourage them to explore what is happening for them in relation to the comments of their children. Perhaps the school counsellor can be a support in this. If the teacher is clear about the importance of this issue and has no discomfort, resolution for the parent should be possible in some way or other.

Because the subject of death and anything related to it **is** so threatening in our society, and there will be parents and others who disapprove of the actions of teachers who follow my suggestions, it is important to have a supervisor or another member of the team as a support in this aspect of the work. That person may need to be involved in discussions with parents who present with difficulties about the way death is handled at school.

Because the subject of this book has been the death of a parent and the resulting grief of the young child, I have addressed this particular loss almost exclusively. All that I have said, however, relates to any kind of loss. As

teachers and child-care workers you will also be presented
with the loss involved for children, and for yourself, when
the children move on to another class or school, or you
move to something else.

At the time of writing, Evania's teacher in her first year
at school is about to leave to have a baby and Ketorah is
about to leave the pre-school she has been attending for
one day each week. These are the losses we need to be
alert to, as well as the changes which occur at the end of
each year.

When such a loss is imminent the teacher or child-care
worker has an excellent opportunity and a responsibility
to prepare the child or children for this experience. It is
not something to be announced on the day of departure.
Rather there needs to be some time beforehand when all
concerned can talk about what is soon to change in their
lives. This preparation will lead to a smoother change-
over with less likelihood of unresolved grief becoming part
of the child's emotional life in the future.

May your experience with children in grief be rewarding, leading to growth for yourself as well as for the little
one in your care.

# 16 A new life about to begin

It is 6 April 1990, the second anniversary of David's death. We have been up to the Highway, to the scene of the accident. To the pole nearest the actual spot where he died we attached flowers and drawings done by the children. A sign I had painted, on which was David's name and the date of his death, had also a rainbow, a symbol of hope.

I had not anticipated completing this little book for many months and it is truly amazing that I should be writing these last words of it on this particular day.

I trust, dear reader, that you have found something that is helpful to you in the sharing of our experience.

Remember that you do not have to 'do it on your own'. Your friends, members of your family, and your neighbours all have different resources to offer your children and it would be indeed tragic if you were to deny your children these through some false attitude about having to meet all your children's needs yourself.

Of course, as well as denying the children, you would be denying yourself the sharing of the responsibility and care of your little ones.

It is enriching for others to be able to spend time with your children, especially close friends who long to be able to contribute something to your lives. So draw on others for support with your children. Draw on the strength and wisdom of your baby or child.

Above all trust yourself in the process. Do not hesitate to seek help when you need it, practical help and that of someone who can support you in your inner work.

This is an unspeakably difficult time for you now.

It is also a time of transition.

For those of you who have given birth 'naturally', you will know that what is called the transition phase of labour is a time of near insanity. And it heralds the imminent birth of your baby.

This transition period after the death of your partner is such a time. Hold on to that fact. There **will** be healing. There **will** be a new life, a new beginning for you all. A new life **is** about to begin. It is perfectly all right if you do not feel that or see it at the moment. Do not struggle to make it so. It will happen. Know only THAT IT WILL.

In the meantime be faithful to your process and that of your little ones.

For myself, the writing of this book has indeed been a great gift. There have been, as expected, tears and times of feeling 'low'. More than that, there has been a sense of strength and clarity and excitement about the future, yours and ours.

So now as you continue your journey, may it be one of great blessedness, with the assurance of our love and blessing as you travel.

# Further reading

The following list of books for further reading will provide you with a starting point. The books on this list have bibliographies which will lead you to other material. With one or two exceptions, these are books I have read myself and consider to be helpful. The comments are specifically directed to the readers of this book.

Any of the works of **Elisabeth Kubler-Ross** are well worth reading. Those mentioned below are books I found particularly helpful in the months following David's death. Do not limit your reading to these only!

Kubler-Ross, Elisabeth. *A Letter to a Child With Cancer* (the Dougy Letter). Available from Elisabeth Kubler-Ross Association (Australia) Limited, PO Leppington, NSW 2171.

This is, as the title suggests, a letter written by Elisabeth to a nine-year-old child who is dying. It is a reproduction of the actual letter and addresses the questions asked by the young boy—'What is life? What is death? Why do young children have to die?' I found this little letter helpful in formulating my own answers to such questions.

Kubler-Ross, Elisabeth. *Remember the Secret*. Celestial Arts, Berkeley, California, 1982.

A beautifully illustrated book for children, it is a story which presents the issue of death to the young readers. The moving story contains hope as well as sadness. I found this particularly relevant to David's older two children and we often cried our way through it when together.

Kubler-Ross, Elizabeth. *On Children and Death.* MacMillan, UK and New York, 1983.

In this book Elisabeth Kubler-Ross speaks directly to the parents of dying children and those whose children have died suddenly, encouraging a creative approach to their situation. It is helpful to read about the children's feelings and comments about death. The chapter about the spiritual awareness of children in relation to death is interesting and helpful to parents who are supporting children in grief.

Kubler-Ross, Elisabeth and Warshaw, Mal. *To Live Until We Say Goodbye.* Prentice-Hall, Englewood Cliffs, NJ, 1978.

These examples of making creative use of what time there is left to someone who is dying, and to those who are close to the dying person, are inspirational. They point us to the importance of **living** no matter what our circumstances, despite the suffering we may be experiencing.

Kubler-Ross, Elisabeth. *Death The Final Stage of Growth.* Simon and Schuster, New York, 1975.

Another valuable work of Elisabeth Kubler-Ross. Contributions are made by ministers, rabbis, doctors, nurses and sociologists and others whose work takes them close to death and the survivors. I read this book a few months before David died and as a result of reading about how death is dealt with in other cultures was more able and confident to have something other than the traditional funeral.

Job, Peg. *The Dying.* Women's Redress Press Inc., PO Box 655, Broadway, NSW 2007, 1986.

This is a moving account of the writer's experience leading up to the death, through cancer, of her husband. Peg Job had young children, including a baby of a few months. I found it particularly interesting to read of the issues worked through by the writer in the time before her husband's death. They were issues with which I was struggling in the months following David's death.

Levine, Stephen. *Who Dies? An Investigation of Conscious Living and Conscious Dying.* Anchor Books, Doubleday, New York, 1982.

Stephen Levine, who has worked with Elisabeth Kubler-Ross, writes in depth about the inner work involved in living our lives more consciously and in so doing being more prepared for conscious dying. His book includes very useful meditations, such as 'Letting go' ... 'Self-forgiveness' ... 'On grief'. In terms of active assistance on my inner journey, his is one of the most helpful books I have read. It increases understanding and awareness in relation to life and death. Highly recommended.

Levine, Stephen. *Healing into Life and Death.* Gateway Books, Bath, UK, 1987.

This book expands some of what is written about in the previous book. Again there are helpful guided meditations to use as tools to aid the inner process. We all need healing of some kind. Unresolved grief from long ago or more recently is one of the areas in which we need healing. Another is in the area of self-acceptance. A forgiveness meditation is especially powerful and there are other exercises to assist us in the healing process.

Kalff, Dora M. *Sandplay: A Phychotherapeutic Approach to the Psyche.* Sigo Press, Boston, 1980.

A series of case studies where sandplay has been used forms the substance of this book. Regarded as a classic, it is one of the few contributions about sandplay in the literature.

Weinrib, Estelle L. *Images of the Self: The Sandplay Therapy Process.* Sigo Press, Boston, 1983.

This excellent book explores the theory as well as practice of sandplay therapy. It is readable and very useful.

Axline, Virginia. M. *Dibs: In Search of Self. Personality Development in Play Therapy.* Penguin, London, 1964.

A much-used little book in our house, this tells the story of a little boy's journey out of almost complete withdrawal from those around him. Virginia Axline as his therapist used play and sandplay as tools to support his journey towards wholeness. It is a very moving story and provides an excellent example of the possibilities of sandplay and play therapies.

Axline, Virginia M. *Play Therapy.* Churchill Livingstone, Edinburgh, 1989.

This is the 'classic' in play therapy, a more academic and thorough discussion of the work that can be done with children, using play.

Rudolph, Marguerita. *Should the Children Know? Talking to Young Children about Death.* Dove Communications, Melbourne, Australia, 1978; Schocken, New York.

This little book is an account and discussion of the issues involved for parents, teacher and children when one of the children in the pre-school died. The writer is the teacher involved. The issues discussed are those we will all face if we have any contact with children at all.

Edwards, Hazel. *I Thought I was the Only One: Coping with Grief and Loss in Schools*. Collins Dove, Melbourne, Australia 1992.

I could hardly contain my excitement when reading this book. It is a book which should be in every teacher's resource file. The writer uses drama as a tool for education, and resolution of grief in the classroom. The book has a section headed 'Coping with grief at school', covering some very practical issues such as a letter from a Principal to parents of a student who has died. The issues faced in a school situation are discussed with sensitivity and clarity. Practical suggestions are very helpful. The other major section includes scriptwriting, actual scripts and activities related to the scripts and points for discussion. Written for primary school children, I am sure this will be of enormous help to anyone involved with groups of children.

Oaklander, Violet. *Windows to Our Children. A Gestalt Therapy Approach to Children and Adolescents*. The Centre for Gestalt Development Inc., New York, 1988.

The ways of working with children discussed here are almost limitless and the writer provides us with a reference book to delve into time and again. Some of the tools discussed include fantasy, drawing, creating things with clay, wood, collage. Story-telling, poetry and puppets are used in her work. The writer adds sensory experience, drama, play therapy and sandplay to the list. Finally there is discussion about specific behaviour problems. Certainly a book worthy of a place on your shelves if you are interested in working with children.

Pearson, Mark and Nolan, Patricia. *Emotional First-Aid for Children: Emotional Release Exercises and Inner-Life Skills. A Practical Guide For Parents, Teachers and Counsellors*. Butterfly Books, Springwood, Australia, 1991.

This is an invaluable aid to working with children. The processes or exercises used make possible access to deep inner material in non-threatening ways. The tools used include drawing, body-outline stencils, tactile processes, and games which use bio-energetics, breath, sound and birthing. Attention is drawn to the use of dance, massage, meditation, symbolism. The latter includes a section on sandplay. The book is set out clearly and is very readable and easy to use. It is indeed a book which I highly recommend to anyone interested in working toward healing in the inner lives of children. Some of the exercises can be modified for use with very young children and others will give you ideas for creating something more appropriate.

Symes, Mary. *Grief and Dreams*. Rene Gordon, North Balwyn, Australia, 1987.

A mother of two small children, Mary Symes became a widow as a result of a yachting accident. She writes of her life after the death of her husband, with particular reference to the way she used her dreams to assist in her process. For parents in a similar situation there is much with which to identify. As well it provides an insight into the use of dreams in the inner work.

Lord, Janice Harris. *No Time for Goodbyes*. Millennium Books, New Town, New South Wales, Australia, 1988 (first published in the US by Pathfinder Publishing, 1987).

This book has been written with particular reference to

the bereaved following a sudden death, where there was, as the title suggests, no time to say goodbye to the one who died. There are accounts of the experiences of people in such situations and some basic suggestions about how to deal with a sudden death.

De Saint-Exupery, Antoine. *The Little Prince.* Piper Books in association with Heinemann, London, 1945; Harcourt Brace Jovanovich, San Diego.

This little parable is too valuable to be categorised simply as a children's book. It should be in the library of every household.

Furth, Gregg M. *The Secret World of Drawings: Healing Through Art.* Sigo Press, Boston, 1988.

This is a most valuable reference book if you have contact with children and are at all interested in their inner life. It is very readable and the reproductions of the drawings discussed are excellent. Gregg Furth has worked with Elisabeth Kubler-Ross and is well known for his work with dying children. You do not have to be a pscho-analyst to appreciate the writer's work. This book is highly recommended.

McMurray, Madeline. *Illuminations—The Healing Image.* Wingbow Press, Berkeley, California, 1988.

The writer leads us to getting in touch with the 'inner artist' we can then call upon to assist us on our inner journey. It is a very practical book with exercises to do using various materials. I have found it most helpful for myself and for others and will continue to 'dip into' it.

Clarke, Jack. *Life After Grief—A Soul Journey After Suicide.* Personal Pathways Press, Georgia, 1989.

This is the only autobiographical account of the grieving

process written by a man I have been able to find. For that reason alone it is worth reading. The writer's wife died through suicide and he writes of his struggle following her death and the subsequent healing and rebuilding of his life.

Manning, Doug. *Don't Take My Grief Away: What to Do When You Lose a Loved One.* Harper and Row, Publishers, San Francisco, 1984.

The writer, a pastor, wrote this book so that he could leave it with those he called upon immediately following the death of someone in the family. It is written with care and sensitivity and includes some very practical information and advice, about the funeral, for example, in the first section. The remaining part of the book, which the writer suggests be read 'a little later', covers many of the issues faced by someone in acute grief. The overwhelming sense of caring in this book will in itself be comforting and the content lead the reader on towards healing.

Manning, Doug. *Comforting Those Who Grieve, A Guide for Helping Others.* Harper and Row, Publishers, San Francisco, 1987.

This little book is written for the ministers and pastors who meet with those in grief and will be helpful to anyone involved with the bereaved in those early days following the death of a loved one. It is particularly relevant to readers from a Christian background.

Panuthos, Claudia and Romeo, Catherine. *Ended Beginnings—Healing Childbearing Losses.* Bergin and Garvey Publishers, Massachusetts, 1984.

This book has just reached my desk and I have not yet read it thoroughly. It appears to be worthwhile especially as it is one of the few books which give practical ways of dealing with grief. It is relevant to all in grief, not only those who have a childbirth loss. There is a chapter giving suggestions for helping children in grief.

Crook, Rae. *Relaxation for Children.* Second Back Row Press, Katoomba, Australia, 1988.
I have recently rediscovered this little book and look forward to using the material in it with my own children. It includes meditation, visualisation, various forms of massage, mandala drawings and classroom work.

Garth, Maureen. *Starbright: Meditations for Young Children.* Collins Dove, Melbourne, Australia, 1991; Harper Collins, San Francisco, USA.
This is an excellent book which has very recently come my way and I look forward to using it with my own children. The imagery in its beauty and simplicity will lead children (and I suspect the adults who read the meditations to the children) into a peaceful dream-filled sleep. The images include animals, ants, trees, river, canoe, as well as the more heavenward images of stars, clouds, birds, butterflies, bees. It is a delightful book and one which is easy to use and will I am sure be much-used in our family and my work with other children.

Rickard, Jenny. *Relaxation for Children: A Handbook for Teachers.* Collins Dove, Melbourne, Australia, 1992.
This is a very practical book. It is indeed as the title suggest, a handbook, and sets out very clearly what the teacher needs to have as resource material and how the quiet time or relaxation period is to be led. The ideas can also be used by parents and others.

Cirlot, J. E. *Dictionary of Symbols*. Routledge and Kegan Paul, London, 1962.

If you are interested in working with symbols in your life, this dictionary is an important aide. There are other dictionaries of symbols but one needs to be cautious in selecting one. This one is a well-known and recommended work.

Chetwynd, Tom. *A Dictionary of Symbols*. Paladin Grafton Books, London, 1982.

Another very useful book for learning about and understanding the symbols in your life.

Reading fairy tales will assist in the understanding of symbolism.

# Sources of possible assistance

The following list is intended as a starting point from which to find someone appropriate for your needs. As far as I could determine, the information was correct at the time of going to print. If you do not reach the organisation you want, telephone directory assistance should be able to provide the current number.

I include a brief introduction to the organisations with whom I have made personal contact and feel confident in recommending them. Sources of help in the USA are given on page 123.

If you are overwhelmed by the thought of 'phoning around' perhaps ask a friend to do the initial phoning for you. He or she can then discuss the findings with you and help you to decide which avenue of help will be most appropriate. Keep handy the phone numbers of the 24-hour phone services so that you do not have to go hunting for them when feeling desperate to talk to someone.

If you feel uncomfortable with the person to whom you are referred, say so and ask to be referred to someone else. This may not be an easy thing to do. Perhaps a friend could liaise with the agency for you. But it is most important that you do not 'put up with' something which is not helpful. It is not your responsibility to remain in the relationship with the helping person in order to make him or her feel good! In most instances the helping person will support you in finding someone else. If he or she is not supportive, this confirms the need for you to find another source of help.

## Australian organisations

### NALAG — National Association for Loss and Grief

NALAG was formed after the Granville (New South Wales) train disaster in 1977 to facilitate the sharing of information and support for professionals who assist the victims of such tragedies and their families. It is now established in each state and its aims are to encourage and promote education in the areas of loss and grief, to provide direct assistance to those suffering loss and grief and to encourage investigation and research into these areas.

A newsletter is prepared for members and includes articles which are practical and helpful as well as information about events in the NALAG calendar and book reviews.

This organisation will be particularly helpful for professionals.

### The Compassionate Friends

This organisation grew out of the support two sets of parents were able to give each other when their respective sons died in the same hospital in England in 1968. It is a support group for the parents of children who have died whether at a young age or not-so-young, in recent times or in the long-distant past. The bereaved parents meet to share their grief and their hope for the future.

A twenty-four-hour telephone service is provided for people who need a supportive person to talk to, someone who has experienced the loss of one of their children. There are also groups of bereaved siblings, the brothers and sisters of those who have died. Such peer group support would seem to me to be particularly relevant for adolescents.

Once again an interesting newsletter is sent to members and a varied selection of helpful pamphlets are available.

## Solace
This self-support group is for those who have lost a partner through death. There are weekly meetings in capital cities and in some country areas where bereaved partners share their grief, are helped to understand the grief process and to find ways of rebuilding their lives. Trained support workers are able to refer where necessary to professional help.

## The Elisabeth Kubler-Ross Association
Elisabeth Kubler-Ross is a pioneer in work with the dying and the bereaved and has written numerous books on the subject. The Association which supports her work organises workshops in Australia each year. The Life, Death and Transition workshops are designed to help participants discover and resolve areas of grief in their lives, and are conducted by people trained by Elisabeth. The Association also has literature, cassettes and videos on the subject and an interesting newsletter is sent to members. Although based in Sydney, this organisation is relevant to any person in grief, and those supporting them, wherever they live in Australia.

PO Leppington NSW 2171       (02) 606 5241.

## National Youthline
(008) 251 008 from anywhere in Australia.

# Adelaide

### Adelaide Citizens Advice Bureau
2nd Floor
44 Pirie Street
Adelaide SA 5000                    (08) 212 4070

### Lifeline
Mission House
10 Pitt Street                         (08) 212 3444
Adelaide SA 5000          Reverse-charge calls accepted

## Compassionate Friends of Adelaide
9 Carlisle Avenue
Morphettville SA 5043       (08) 294 1725

## Solace Association of SA
189 Unley Road
Unley SA 5061       (08) 272 4334

## NALAG National Association for Loss and Grief
21 Caroline Street
Flagstaff Hill SA 5159       (08) 275 9911

## PALS Parental Adult Loss Support Inc
60 Greenwillow Drive
Happy Valley SA 5159       (08) 371 1009

## Bereavement Through Suicide Support Group
PO Box 151
Norwood SA 5067       (08) 272 9538
      (08) 332 2696

## SANDS Stillbirth and Neonatal Death Support Association
Marion Community House
887 Marion Road
Mitchell Park SA 5043       (08) 277 0304

## SIDS Sudden Infant Death Syndrome
301 Payneham Road
Royston Park SA 5070       (08) 363 1963
      (08) 263 5403 AH

# Melbourne

## CAB Citizens Advice Bureau
Swanston Street
Melbourne Vic 3000       (03) 650 1062

## Lifeline
148 Lonsdale Street
Melbourne Vic 3000       (03) 662 1000

## Compassionate Friends
205 Blackburn Road
Syndal Vic 3149       (03) 802 8222

## NALAG National Association for Loss and Grief
PO Box 64
Footscray Vic 3011       (03) 688 4760

## Bereaved Parent Centre
205 Blackburn Road
Syndal Vic 3149       (03) 802 8151

## Chesed Jewish Bereavement Support
133 Hawthorn Road
Caulfield North Vic 3161       (03) 528 2273

## Griefline
476 Kooyong Road
Caulfield South Vic 3162       (03) 596 7799

## SIDS Sudden Infant Death Syndrome
1227 Malvern Road
Malvern Vic 3144       (03) 822 9611

# Brisbane

## Association of Civilian Widows
239 Gregory Terrace
Brisbane Qld 4000       (07) 831 5810

## CAB Citizens Advice Bureau
Brisbane Administration Centre
69 Ann Street
Brisbane Qld 4000       (07) 221 4343
      (07) 229 5798

## Lifeline Brisbane
16 Hamilton Place
Bowen Hills Qld 4006       (07) 252 1213

## SANDS Stillbirth and Neonatal Death Support Association
3 Claremont Street
Thorneside Qld 4158       (07) 207 1397

## SIDS Sudden Infant Death Syndrome
7 Morgan Road
Norman Park Qld 4170       (07) 395 6078

**NALAG National Association for Loss and Grief**
15 Garnet Avenue
Kallangur Qld 4503          (07) 881 1505

**Compassionate Friends**
PO Box 218
Springwood Qld 4127          (07) 252 7546

**Solace**
(07) 366 2998
(07) 398 1972

**Beginning Experience** — a support group for the widowed, separated and divorced
(075) 32 2923

# Perth

**CAB Citizens Advice Bureau**
First floor
Law Society House
33 Barrack Street
Perth WA 6000          (09) 221 5711

**Compassionate Friends**
Room 201
79 Sterling Street
Perth WA 6000          (09) 227 5698

**Solace**
333 William Street
Perth WA 6000          (09) 332 5863

**NALAG National Association for Loss and Grief**
Kingswood College
Hampden Road
Crawley WA 6009          (09) 470 5109

**SANDS Stillbirth and Neonatal Death Support Service**
King Edward Memorial Hospital     (09) 382 2687

**Tragic Loss Support Group**
Rheola
West Perth WA 6005          (09) 382 1051

## Western Institute of Self Help
80 Railway Street
Cottesloe WA 6011        (09) 383 3188

## SIDS Sudden Infant Death Syndrome
33 Sixth Avenue
Kensington WA 6151        (09) 474 3544

# Sydney

## Lifeline
Level 3
11–13 Wilmot Street
Sydney NSW 2000        (02) 264 2222

## NALAG National Association for Loss and Grief
PO Box 79
Turramurra NSW 2074        (02) 449 5279

## Compassionate Friends
3rd Floor
381 Pitt Street
Sydney NSW 2000        (02) 267 6962

## Solace
       (02) 451 2891

## Outstretched Hand Foundation — printing and distribution of leaflets about various issues relating to life-threatening illness, dying and bereavement
12 East Market Street
Richmond NSW 2753        (018) 410 535

## The Elisabeth Kubler-Ross Association
PO Leppington NSW 2171        (02) 606 5241

## SIDS Sudden Infant Death Society
36 Toolang Road
St Ives NSW 2075        (02) 446 128

## Bereavement CARE Centre
41 The Boulevarde
Lewisham NSW 2049        (02) 569 9311

**Salvo Careline**
339 Crown Street
Surry Hills NSW 2010      (02) 331 600
                                   (24 hours)

# Hobart

**CAB Citizens Advice Bureau**
Eastlands Shopping Square
Rosny Park Tas 7018      (002) 440 671

**Lifeline**
160 New Town Road
New Town Tas 7008      (002) 345 600

**SIDS Sudden Infant Death Syndrome**
190 Macquarie Street
Hobart Tas 7000      (002) 342 601

**Compassionate Friends**
277 Carlton Beach Road
Carlton Beach Tas 7173      (002) 659 183

**Solace**
Senior Citizens Centre
Bathurst Street
Hobart Tas 7000      (002) 438 620

**HOLD Helping Ourselves and Others**
Hospice Care Association
The Coach House
St Johns Hospital      (022) 235 044

**Lady Gowrie Support Services**
17 Runnymede Street
Battery Point Tas 7004      (002) 349 833

**SANDS Stillbirth and Neonatal Death
Support Association**
     (002) 435 464

**NALAG National Association for Loss and Grief**
33 Cromwell Street
Battery Point Tas 7004      (002) 237 474

## Darwin

**Citizens Advice Bureau** equivalent
Community Information Officer
Casuarina Public Library
Bradshaw Terrace
Casuarina NT 0810

**CRADLE** (a similar organisation to SIDS and SANDS)
C/o Darwin Private Hospital
PO Box 42571
Casuarina NT 0811                    (089) 206 010

**SIDS Sudden Infant Death Network of NT**
PO Box 314
Sanderson NT 0812                    (089) 272 923

**Somerville Community Services —**
**Family Support Services**
PO Box 42644
Casuarina NT 8011                    (089) 451 533 Cas
                                     (089) 323 096 Palm

**Crisisline**
                (089) 819 227
                (008) 019 116

## Alice Springs NT

For information about sources of help contact the Community Information officer (089) 522 733 extension 244.

## Katherine NT

For information about sources of help contact the Community Information Officer (089) 711 313.

## Specifically Practical Help

**Home Care** or an equivalent agency can provide help with the domestic tasks, shopping and cooking and sometimes essential home maintenance. Fees are adjusted according to ability to pay.

Contact your local Council for information regarding the service in your area.

**Day Care Centres** can provide occasional and regular care of your young children. Check the phone book for centres near you, the local council or your state equivalent of a Community Welfare Department, Family or Children's Services. Fees are based on your income with government subsidy for all but those on high incomes.

**Family Day Care** where children are cared for in the home of the carer who is usually a mother with young children of her own. The phone book will once again lead you to them, or the local council or state Family and Community Services Department or the equivalent. Fees are based on your ability to pay.

**Dial an Angel** provides domestic help and a range of related services. For our purposes, however, the most relevant is the **nanny** service which can be short- or long-term, live-in or daily, a few hours or full-time.

We have used this agency in three states and I recommend it. Cost is a standard hourly, daily or weekly rate.

## Unites States Organisations

### The Elisabeth Kubler-Ross Center

A non-profit, non-sectarian organisation dedicated to the enhancement of life and growth through the practice of unconditional love. There are support groups, called Friends of Elisabeth Kubler-Ross, in most states. Call the Center for more information.

South Route 616
Head Waters Virginia 24442     (703) 396 3441

## Compassionate Friends

The Compassionate Friends is a mutual assistance self-help organisation offering friendship and understanding to bereaved parents and siblings. The primary purpose is to assist them in the positive resolution of the grief experienced upon the death of a child and to support their efforts to achieve physical and emotional health. There are 660 chapters throughout the United States.

PO Box 3696
Oak Brook
Illinois 60522-3696                    (708) 990 0100

## The Good Grief Program

The Good Grief Program helps schools and community groups become a base of support for children when a friend dies.

Judge Baker Children's Center
295 Longwood Avenue
Boston Massachusetts 02115

## The Life Center of the Suncoats Inc.

The Life Center is an organisation dedicated to providing free counselling, education and group support to people experiencing the stresses associated with serious or life-threatening illness or loss due to the death of a loved one.

214 S. Fielding Avenue
Tampa Florida 33606                    (813) 251 0289

## Pregnancy and Infant Loss Center

For bereaved families experiencing miscarriage, stillbirth and infant death.

(612) 473 9372

## SIDS

Sudden Infant Death Syndrome Alliance
10500 Little Patuxent Parkway
Suite 420                              (800) 221 7437
Columbia Maryland 21044                (410) 964 8000